UNCENSORED CELEBRITIES

UNCENSORED
CELEBRITIES

by

EDWARD RAYMOND THOMPSON
(E. T. RAYMOND, pseud.)

Essay Index Reprint Series

 BOOKS FOR LIBRARIES PRESS
FREEPORT, NEW YORK

First Published 1919
Reprinted 1970

STANDARD BOOK NUMBER:
8369-1687-5

LIBRARY OF CONGRESS CATALOG CARD NUMBER:
71-117855

PRINTED IN THE UNITED STATES OF AMERICA

PREFACE

IN the political world, as in all others, the war has created new standards, and the following sketches, slight though they be, are designed to assist the process of revaluation.

They are not meant for the hero-worshipper. The Hero as Politician, always rare, is not discoverable just now by the present writer. "THE MAN" of the newspaper articles has still to appear, though he has been regularly announced every three months or so. For the most part one can only say of political things that they have got themselves transacted somehow. But while, like the angry ape, certain politicians have played "fantastic tricks before high heaven," others have emerged with credit from the supreme test, and still others have meant exceedingly well.

In his task of classification the author has paid scant attention to party labels, and has always preferred the wider to the narrower loyalty. The most important question to be asked of any public man at this time, "Is he a good Englishman?" cannot be resolved by purely intellectual tests. Judge Jeffreys used to say that he could "smell" a certain kind of person "a mile off.'' The present writer can claim no such delicacy of perception ; yet he is not ashamed to admit that in some doubtful cases he has relied chiefly on his nose.

CONTENTS

UNCENSORED CELEBRITIES

MR. LLOYD GEORGE

It is not very material to this or any other generation that Mr. Lloyd George has been "filmed." But posterity, in its study of this time, will be grateful that he has been painted by a man of genius.

To our successors most that has been written concerning this eminent man must make for sheer bewilderment. It is "hot ice and wondrous strange snow." They will read of a white negro, a dwarf ten feet high, a demagogue who tyrannized over the mob, a sycophant who bullied and plundered the rich. Many quite rational people believe that Shakespeare never wrote the plays and sonnets simply because the only dependable portrait of him is that mournful Droeshout engraving showing what Gainsborough called "as damned stupid a head as ever I saw." What degree of misjudgment might not be possible to men examining, after the lapse of centuries, a newspaper illustration of Mr. George opening a bazaar or patting an election baby?

But Mr. Augustus John's notable canvas will tend to avoidance of the grosser kind of error concerning Mr. Lloyd George's character. Just as the painting of Vandyke tells us more about the essential Strafford than all the careful pages of Clarendon, so this remarkable study reveals the true personality of Mr. George better than many volumes of Hansard and the Parliamentary sketch-writers. In regarding it one begins to understand why the subject stands where he is to-day. One realizes for the first time that there is great

9

strength in the man. Physical strength first, despite the lack of inches : sturdy build, bull neck, powerful shoulders, the whole man approximating to that southern European type which produces the greatest masters of swordsmanship, a type that surprises in the test of battle those northerners who are prone to over-value mere stature. One feels that in other times and other circumstances the owner of this physique might have fought many duels and yet died in his bed. As things are one is not surprised to learn that he bears fatigue easily, can sleep anywhere and at any time, and is not readily daunted by difficulties, so long as they challenge his interest. In the features can be read an inflexibility of purpose compatible with infinite pliability of method; an impatience of opposition; even a certain ruthlessness—one of the abler Roman Emperors of the later period, from Illyria or Spain, might have had much such a face. It is not the face of a great master of statecraft; the brain behind those rather sceptical and mocking eyes is quick and vigor-ous, but neither capacious nor subtle; it enjoys an intellectual game of draughts, but chess is rather beyond it. Still, so far as they see, the eyes see clearly, and the brain, within its limits, is an admir-able instrument. For the special purposes of its owner, perhaps as good an instrument as he could have.

For Mr. Lloyd George belongs essentially to the empirical school of statesmanship. He does not look "before and after," but only about him. He stands in small awe of precedent, principle, and doctrine; he is always readier to experiment than to think. In-tensely interested in the things of the moment, in himself and the people he likes, in the "causes" which appeal to him in his varying moods, no man has less sense of the continuity of human things. For him the present tick of the clock has all the dignity of the eternal. He is, in truth, as much a man of action as any foxhunter of the shires or any leader of a forlorn hope. Withal there is in him something of the poet; he has a touch of the true Promethean fire, and only when he is very tired does the coin from his phrase-mint ring tinny. Occasionally, like the German Emperor, whom he somewhat resembles in his knack of saying memorable things on trivial occasions (as well, it must be added, as trivial things on some memorable occasions), he rises to very considerable heights; if the Victorian book-making fashion still held, a very tolerable collection of " Beauties " could be made from his speeches. But, though he keenly enjoys his gift of eloquent utterance, and sometimes takes a more languid pleasure in the eloquence of others, words are for him only missiles and munitions, better or worse; the fight is the main thing. The fever of doing, the gust and passion of perpetual movement, the revolt against passivity, are in his very blood. If thought is a malady, he is of all men most healthy. His poor acquaintance with history and literature are less the consequence of lack of opportunity than of his innate dislike of hard study. He is in a sense indolent through excess of energy. What can be done at a sitting he does as well as most men; but he quickly tires of monotonous application, and his only idea of repose is change of effort. Hence the just criticism that he raises many questions and settles few, that whatever he touches he leaves a litter for some less gifted person to clear up, and that the more passionately he advocates a policy the less he can be trusted to carry it to its logical conclusion.

The energy was no doubt inborn; the lack of discipline may be partly traceable to the desultory education to which he was condemned by the failure and early death of his father. He is fond of referring to himself as a child of the people, and his enemies used to speak of him as an essentially cultureless man.

Both descriptions are misleading. Mr. Lloyd George belongs to a class with a social pride no less highly developed than that of the heraldic gentleman. His grandfather and father were both entirely " respectable "—the former a yeoman farmer and the latter a schoolmaster who narrowly missed the ministry. Half the peerage might search in vain for as creditable a beginning of their family trees. It was accident, and not birth, that threw the infant George among the poor. There is a curious resemblance between his early life and that of Charles Dickens, and a parallel might be drawn, not inappropriately, between the effects of precocious experience of misfortune on these two men. Had John Dickens been a success, Charles would have found life smoothed for him by school, university, and the rest; he would doubtless have gone to the Bar or passed into the higher Civil Service, and would have ended the usual " brilliant career " in knighted and pensioned ease. But John Dickens made shipwreck of everything, and Charles, with his vivid nature and wounded middle-class pride, filled bottles with blacking and his soul with bitterness. To the end of his days he was haughtily conscious of the outrage, and let it envenom every dart of satire he hurled against English society. What would have happened had the paternal George lived to coach his son for scholarships, despatch him cheaply to Oxford, and throw the necessary monetary sop to the Inner Temple or Gray's Inn Cerberus? Probably Mr. George would have still entered politics, but it would have been as an Asquith or a Simon, fundamentally satisfied with things as they are, and " except in opinion not disagreeing " with his late enemies the Dukes.

As things were, he started the world without what is called education, but with such substitute as a lad of quick parts and vivid temperament may pick up at a village school and from the conversation of his elders. Such disadvantages may be easily over-estimated. There are many worse tutors than the village shoemaker who was his uncle and second father; and it may be doubted whether the Oxford Union offers a better training for the embryo politician than the debating circle of a Welsh Nonconformist chapel. At any rate young George scraped together enough information to qualify as a solicitor at the age of twenty-one; he became a practised speaker in two languages before he had need of a razor; and at fifteen he knew more of the realities of life than most men do at thirty. He was not, and is not, possessed of formal culture. But many of the greatest scholars have had smaller opportunity. If he learned only what was immediately necessary for his purpose the fault was mainly his; application, as has been already noted, was painful to him, and what could not be picked up sparrow fashion he never acquired. But to speak of such a man as " uneducated " is merely snobbish.

It is in that last word that we have the secret of much. In America a politician thus " raised " and instructed would feel no sort of handicap, and nobody would feel it for him. If he did not know one set of facts, what matter? There are too many facts for one man to know. Education of any kind is to the purpose : mode and place of education matter little. But in this country schools and universities, though in some incidental way concerned with education, are very much more concerned with another thing. They aim chiefly at manufacturing gentlemen. In this age of progress we have only negatively improved on the ideal of the great Dr. Arnold. His scheme was for the multiplication of " Christian gentlemen "; we have dropped the adjective and intensified the substantive. Otherwise Arnold's theory holds in all its massive simplicity. Against the undoubted advantages of this view is to be set one trifling drawback.

A certain number of quite talented young men constantly fail, from some reason or another, to receive the recognized hall-mark of good form, and, according to their natures, resent the fact either lazily or vehemently. Some run to satire, more or less good-humoured; some take up a fiercely hostile attitude to the established order of things. There are few men—and very few Englishmen—so philosophical as to be indifferent whether they are thought gentlemen, and the most sensitive of all are those who, well educated "privately," find a subtle barrier between themselves and the men of Balliol or Trinity. They are snobs, of course, to trouble about the matter; but they would not trouble about it but for the general snobbery.

The mischief operates in two directions. It breeds not only an irritation which sometimes takes distinctly anti-social forms, but an involuntary over-estimation of academic and social advantages which not seldom leads the tribune of the plebs, once arrived at power, to yield undue homage to great wealth and settled position. The same man who declaims against privilege in the abstract is apt to be overflattered when privilege in the concrete invites him to a country-house week-end.

It may be doubted whether Mr. Lloyd George was much troubled by his educational or social limitations when he entered Parliament at twenty-seven for Carnarvon. His rebellion then was against something less subtle : something personified by the squire of his district and the parson of his parish. But as he gradually ceased to be a Welsh Nationalist and developed into an English Radical there can be little doubt that an additional touch of venom was imparted to his attacks on the "gentlemanly party" by the fact that it was so very gentlemanly. Though Joseph Chamberlain was the chief object of his youthful fury, it was not against him but against the grandees of Conservatism proper that the real vendetta existed. Mr. Lloyd George no doubt felt much of the passion he expressed during the Boer War; one of the finest features of his character is a hatred of the more theatrical kinds of oppression, and he quite sincerely saw in the warfare of the African republics the resistance of a weak thing in the right to a strong thing in the wrong. He little cared that the Boer had been himself a considerable oppressor. But though he might assail Mr. Chamberlain with every weapon in an armoury that included invective, satire, personal gibe, and imaginative appeal, he could hardly feel against that great man as he did against the hereditary hidalgos. Both he and Chamberlain belonged to the middle class; both were destitute of what is called the higher culture; Chamberlain had made his way, as the young Welshman hoped to make his, by sheer force of ability and character. And if some secret sympathy may have mingled with antagonism even at this period, there was assuredly more when Chamberlain, flinging out of office, started on that last campaign which exhausted his ebbing vitality. Such an act of courage was very much in Mr. George's own way. Besides, he was not quite at home in the battle of the economists. He declaimed rather than argued on stock party lines; it is doubtful whether his mind was so constituted as to understand the deeper issues. Possibly it was fatigue of the Tariff controversy as much as anything that urged him to the great Budget diversion of 1909; during his two years at the Board of Trade he was certainly as silent, and probably as bored, as at any period of his life. But he had made some business reputation in that office. True, he was nothing to boast of as a departmental chief; penny plain business has never attracted him like twopence coloured adventure. He left the permanent staff to manage things much as they liked; he revealed, however, a capacity in negotiation which surprised many who had so far seen in him no more than an unusually clever agitator. But the comparative narrowness of the job irked him, and when Mr. Asquith became Prime Minister it is believed that one of his first difficulties was Mr. George's demand for instant promotion. The new Chief is said to have fancied Mr. McKenna as his successor at the Treasury. But Mr. Lloyd George made it plain that he would be Chancellor of the Exchequer or nothing, and Mr. Asquith could not afford to let him be nothing.

As for Mr. George, he had determined to be something in the most emphatic sense. " I care not who makes my country's laws if I make its songs," said a rather foolish phrase-monger. Mr. George cared not who presided over the Cabinet so long as he made the Budget. He was determined to create a sensation, and he succeeded. The Budget of 1909 was hardly revolutionary; in these days of really " confiscatory taxation " the fierce debate on Mr. George's proposals seems in retrospect theatrical and unreal. But if the Chancellor had really proposed to inscribe the words "National Property" over Chatsworth and Bowood he could have hardly done it with a more apocalyptic air. There is no doubt that he enjoyed the whole thing immensely. He was avenging all the slights of the little Welsh lad, all the stately tolerance of the village attorney, all the polite sneers levelled at the rising politician. Never was public duty so happily wedded to private inclination. There was always something a little feline in Mr. Lloyd George, and he now took a perfectly cat-like pleasure in tearing out the tail feathers of some solemn, gorgeous, jewelled bird, some peacock of the peerage who rasped out denunciations of his wickedness. He rejoiced in his new character as a political Attila or Hammer of God, and positively revelled in what he called the " howls from Belgravia." He shrieked with gay laughter—as who would not?—when told that he would never, no never, be again invited to Blenheim; he drove Lord Rothschild into terrified silence with a single quip. No man in our time has ever enjoyed such extremes of popularity and detestation; it was the mark of good-breeding to vilify him as the " little Welsh solicitor," and in the more select suburbs of London he was known as the " Cad of the Cabinet." All this glory could not last, and if there had been no Insurance Act and no Marconi affair Mr. George's vogue must have suffered some diminution. Still, though his prestige was somewhat dimmed, the outbreak of war found him still the most powerful of British Ministers.

It will probably be many years before the world knows precisely how it came to pass that the most pronounced Pacifist of the Pacifist Liberal Cabinet, the man who had declared that we were " building Dreadnoughts against a phantom," and had but six months before begun a passionate crusade against armaments, sided in the fateful decision of August 4, 1914, against Lord Morley and Mr. Burns and with the Prime Minister and Sir Edward Grey. The fact having been taken for granted, its decisive importance has hardly been enough realized. Opposition to war was far stronger than is generally supposed. The great financial interests were against participation; so far from the war being a " capitalists' war," it was declared in the teeth of the cosmopolitan money kings. A majority of the Cabinet was either unconvinced or lukewarm; the great Quaker supporters of the Ministry were naturally adverse; the " Socialists" were up in arms; even the undeniably patriotic Parliamentary leaders of Labour were deeply distrustful. Had all these elements been united under a leader of genius and great Parliamentary skill, the decision of the Cabinet might well have been in favour of neutrality, or at the best Great Britain would have

2

entered the war a State not only militarily unprepared
but divided against itself. It is idle to give imagination rein as to the conceivable limits of the might-
have-been. But it is hardly fanciful to say that, when
some instinct saved Mr. Lloyd George from a capital
error, it also preserved civilization from a crowning
calamity.

"The ill that's done ye can compute, but never
what's resisted." The same applies to good. Many
may have forgotten, but none can dispute, as none
can estimate with precision, the service Mr. George
rendered to the Allied cause by merely espousing it.
But there is naturally more division of opinion concerning the value of his specific contributions to the
prosecution of the war. The whole question is so
mixed up with personal and party considerations that
it is almost hopeless to look for an impartial judgment
from British men of this generation. Let us, however,
make an effort to view facts as they would appear to
posterity or even to a contemporary foreigner. The
war work of Mr. Lloyd George divides itself roughly
into two periods : his service as a nominally subordinate but exceedingly powerful Minister and his service
as titular head of the Government. During the first
period Mr. Lloyd George was one of three men of
British race who in the political sphere stood out as
world figures; the others were Mr. Asquith and Sir
Edward Grey. There can be no question as to which
of the trio most impressed the imagination of non-
British mankind. Mr. Asquith's words might carry
more weight with a select minority ; Sir Edward Grey's
lightest whisper caused strained attention in every
gathering of official men. But it was Mr. Lloyd
George's voice that reached everywhere the masses;
in France, Italy, the United States, and the British
Dominions he, perhaps the one politician (save Lord
Milner) least typically British, figured as specially the
representative of the British people.

The fact, of course, was due to that extraordinary gift of expression which Mr. Lloyd George has brought to the highest possible pitch of cultivation, while wisely refraining from anything which would spoil its peculiar race and flavour. He has the great advantage of being a real orator in an age when oratory hardly exists. It would be tempting to discuss how it happens that rhetoric, most artificial of the arts, was most assiduously cultivated when Parliament was most real, and has declined with the veracity of Parliament. An off-hand answer would be that statesmen thought it worth while to cultivate the art of persuasive appeal so long as votes might be influenced by speech, but disdain such devices when Whips can inform a Prime Minister long before the event what the result of a division will be, assuming that this group is placated, and that group effectively threatened. Be that as it may, there is no doubt that public speaking, if it had not exactly degenerated, had wholly changed its character before Mr. Lloyd George showed that passionate and compelling rhetoric still counts. A dry and parsimonious manner, of which Mr. Asquith is perhaps the most notable exemplar, was the model for the High Court of Parliament as well as the King's Bench; the style of Burke was as obsolete in the one place as that of Buzfuz in the other. There could be no greater reproach to a Parliamentarian than to class his speaking as florid and " high-faluting." Macaulay described the best Parliamentary oratory as " reason penetrated and made red-hot by passion." In much modern speaking plausibility depends on low temperature; things which would seem wholly mad if declaimed gain a certain appearance of sanity by the moderation of their presentation. It is certain that a languid House of Commons has accepted many measures at the suggestion of a frigid Under-Secretary, and in face of tepidly rational objections, which would have been rejected had they been justified by the stately periods of Pitt and opposed in the spluttering eloquence of Fox.

Mr. Lloyd George has to some degree respected the modern House of Commons humour, but the larger audience of the nation he treats to the full power of his very real eloquence, and, somewhat to its astonishment, the British people finds that, Carlyle notwithstanding, the talker is vastly important. Mr. Lloyd George's talk has been of incalculable service during the war. I am not referring here to his more ambitious efforts of statesmanlike utterance; Mr. Asquith could always reply to a German or Austrian statesman, or to a great neutral, with more weight and dignity. I am thinking rather of speeches addressed straight to the British people, telling them things already familiar, but in tones that vibrated to the very centre of their being. Mr. Asquith could tell the people why they must fight as a duty. Mr. Law could tell them what they would lose by not fighting. Lord Lansdowne could explain why they must fight until the real pinch came. But only the Welsh orator could say a simple thing in this simple but yet enormously effective way :

" We have been living in a sheltered valley for generations. We have been too comfortable and too self-indulgent, many perhaps too selfish, and the stern hand of fate has scourged us to an elevation where we can see the everlasting things that matter—the great peaks we had forgotten, of Duty, Honour, Patriotism, and, clad in glittering white, the towering pinnacle of Sacrifice pointing like a rugged finger to heaven."

Many of these speeches, as one reads them now, cause at once a thrill and a shiver—the thrill because they revive in throbbing reality the emotions of a moment past, the shiver because one thinks for an instant, thanking Heaven for its mercy, what might have been had this power been exercised on the other side. It is a power almost independent of the personality of the orator. Those who most distrust

Mr. George yield to the spell of his eloquence at its best with the facility of his most enslaved admirers. Time and again he has met, in the House of Commons and elsewhere, an audience under the cloud of a great misfortune, sullen, suspicious, unfriendly; hardly ever has he sat down without bringing its mood in harmony with his own. Occasionally he has been tempted, by the consciousness of his power, to abuse it; but on the whole a splendid and unique talent has been well employed.

Of Mr. Lloyd George's purely official activities during the earlier war period it is only possible to speak in general terms. When the whole fabric of finance threatened to topple, large and bold measures were taken by a Treasury of which he was the head. They were justified by their success, and it is worth noting that when it was proposed to remove the Chancellor of the Exchequer to another field the City of London, once bitterly critical, petitioned that he should remain in charge of national finance. His work at the new Ministry of Munitions was a monument to his energy, if cool examination could not fail to detect a good deal of incidental sloppiness in the execution of a grandiose plan. Under his management the department rapidly expanded, and produced and spent (even squandered) on a scale before unimaginable. New industries were created, old industries were adapted, to meet the colossal requirements of war, and undeniably the main object was attained in full measure. If all difficulties were not met, they were at least skilfully dodged; some sort of concordat was established with Labour as to the relaxation of trade union rules impeding production, and though there has been constant friction there has been no absolute breakdown. It is pretty certain that nobody but Mr. Lloyd George would have had the courage to attempt the fifth of what he actually achieved, and that in doing so he sacrificed much of his prestige with a certain "democratic" section to which he had always looked for support must be counted unto him for righteousness.

With Mr. Lloyd George's departure from the Ministry of Munitions the first period of his war administration may be said to end; his tenure of the War Office was featureless, and hardly matters in a review like the present. We now approach the most debatable part of his career—the *coup d'état* of 1916. It can at once be said that the methods employed to displace Mr. Asquith could only be justified on one ground—that of pressing national necessity. "I can save the country, and no other man can," said the elder Pitt; and that is, too, Mr. George's apologia. Established in office, he certainly showed by every action that he possessed illimitable confidence in his power to bring the State through its troubles. He began by a not inconsiderable constitutional revolution : the Cabinet system was destroyed at a blow; the supreme governing power was put in the hands of a knot of men who need not necessarily be members of either House of Parliament or even citizens of the United Kingdom. "Party claims" could not be ignored entirely, but men of "push and go" from great business houses, railways, and elsewhere were recruited for the Ministry. New departments were created with a lavish hand. The control of food, travel, and other necessities of life was vastly extended. Immensely increased demands were made on the manhood of the country, and the cost of the war and the public services mounted sharply. An enormous but rather undisciplined energy pervaded the administration; there was bustle enough; whether bustle was always business was not so clear.

In some respects the new Government had very bad luck, and misfortunes which no skill could have avoided rendered judgment difficult regarding those which derived from want of foresight and co-ordina-

tion. The Russian revolution destroyed all the fair
hopes built on the military position after the Battle
of the Somme. Unrestricted submarine warfare,
while bringing in an ultimately powerful Ally, produced also an immediate situation of the most alarming kind. In the air, as at sea, we were on the defen-
sive, and on land small and transient successes, gained
at great cost, were all that could be set off against
a great disaster like Caporetto. At home the food
troubles grew daily more insistent; and Irish difficulties were accentuated. On the whole, however, it
was plain that the new Government had certain definite
advantages over the old. It was more united as to
its objective; it was in a certain sense what it pro-
claimed itself to be, a "win-the-war" Government.
In discarding elements weary or lukewarm, it had
gained in momentum, and had behind it the energy
of a people with new hope. On the other hand,
evidence was quickly forthcoming of one grave fault,
which is sufficiently indicated in the recurrent cry
for better "co-ordination." The right hand of the
Administration knew too little what the left hand was
doing; and the head seemed to know even less concerning either hand. Ministers were set up with an hotel
and an expensive office establishment and told to make
themselves busy, with such results as were revealed
in the extreme case of the first National Service
experiment. Meanwhile powerful newspaper interests
which had favoured the dismissal of Mr. Asquith
attempted to dictate policy in headlines, and all these
factors combined to give an oddly vacillating character to administration. Certain great things were
achieved; the food troubles were met with success;
and the signal advantage of unity of command,
pursued by somewhat devious means, was at length
attained. But undeniably the new arrangements did
not make for orderliness or economy in the public
service.

The character of the Prime Minister, in brief, was reflected in the character of his Administration. It cannot be a rational complaint that he attacked his work in the only way compatible with his temperament. It is useless to expect a Michael Angelo to have the finish of a Dutch "little master," and Mr. Lloyd George's fancy is all for the "grands contours du dessin"; he recks little of the finishing touches.

He has a quite unusual capacity for getting to the heart of any matter to which his attention is specifically directed; his judgment is shrewd; his courage high; his driving power remarkable. But the very intensity of his nature forbids calm envisagement of things as a whole. He has little faculty for exercising a general command, and his talent for discovering talent, though considerable, is not always allowed full play; the claims of private partiality, political affinity, or convenience and so forth are often given undue weight. Thus he is often badly served, does not discover the fact till too late, and too often fails to correct what is wrong even after it is manifest. Mr. Lloyd George's Ministry is like an orchestra composed of performers of very unequal merit, under a conductor who only occasionally troubles to conduct, being engaged in writing the music, looking after the stage carpentry, advertising the performance, and even selling the tickets. It is not quite an adequate compensation that the conductor himself is a master on many instruments, and can always be relied on to snatch trombone or piccolo from a pretender and show how the thing should be done.

Allowance must be made, however, for many difficulties, from which his predecessor also was not exempt. His efforts to shake himself free from party have not been wholly successful; in that he resembles the man who finds his trouble far from ended by separation from a troublesome wife. Of some of his colleagues one might repeat the French wit's dictum on women : one can't live with them and can't live without them. The scheme by which Mr. George was to supply the ideas and energy, and others the "calm wisdom," was perhaps inherently unworkable; it has not in fact worked. In attending to the only interests about which the public cares, Mr. George has had to keep a watchful eye on interests for which the public cares nothing, but the management of which is essential to the maintenance of his position. He has had to work with many tools he would not have chosen, and, like other tailors, has had to cut his coat to his cloth.

That garment is still in the stage of shreds, thrums, and chalk-marks; it is yet too early to say what will be the final result. In the language of a discarded philosophy, we can only wait and see. But we cannot honestly withhold admiration from much we have seen, even if we have to place limits to our worship. And we wait in a spirit of increasing hope, tempered, perhaps, with some little concern lest at a critical moment audacity should degenerate into recklessness or that the instinct which dictated the right course in 1914 should falter in face of things almost as vital and far more complex.

SIR EDWARD CARSON

I REMEMBER well the afternoon in the early summer of 1915 when the first Coalition Government met an anxious and rather angry House of Commons.

While discarded Ministers gloomed at them from the Speaker's left hand the members of Mr. Asquith's new team made a brave show of coalescing in public. Mr. Long exchanged elaborate civilities with Mr. Birrell. Mr. Bonar Law, with something of the self-

consciousness of a schoolboy presented to the squire
at a prize-giving, tried to be at ease in Zion with Mr.
McKenna. Mr. Harcourt showed princely urbanity
to some understrapper recruit.

It was not very hopeful or convincing. Yet men
did hope. They thought there was a chance for the
Government, and were disposed to give it its chance.

And then something happened that even the visitor
in the Strangers' Gallery could feel, though he might
find it mysterious. A tall, gaunt man entered behind
the Speaker's chair, and perched himself, like Poe's
raven on the bust of Pallas, at the very extremity of
the Treasury Bench. A very ravenlike personage,
black, aloof, and sinister. He spoke to none. He
listlessly turned over the pages of his order paper,
yawned with the easy but terrifying grace of one of
the higher carnivora, surveyed the House with super-
cilious, heavy-lidded eyes, and presently went out.

It was nothing, and yet everything. The coming of
Sir Edward Carson, the new Attorney-General, had
cast a shade which his departure did not remove.
For the sight of that hatchet face—the profile of an
Indian brave, the heavily pomaded black hair combed
back from the low forehead, the dew-lapped eyes, the
humourless, scornful mouth, the projecting Habsburg-
like chin—reminded all but a few how slight was the
chance on which they relied. A few moments ago
the political equation looked hard, indeed, but not
insoluble. But here was the intractable surd that was
bound to complicate everything.

It is just this difficulty at arriving at the square root
of Sir Edward Carson that makes him so interesting
a man and so impossible a politician. Trotsky and
his like are hard enough to understand. Still, they
remain Trotskys. But there have been so many
Carsons. First, as the foundation of all subsequent
Carsons, we have the young ex-Liberal barrister who,
in the days of "resolute government," entered into

the dreary task of repression with a zealot's gusto that almost dignified it. Then come some years of high official rank and emolument; Sir Edward Carson, English Solicitor-General, quietly enjoys the reward of strenuous party service. With the Unionist defeat of 1906 emerges another Carson, for we can almost consider the great advocate of the King's Bench in his best period as different in kind as well as degree from all earlier Carsons. It was not until this time that he showed all his gifts at their fullest—unmatched dexterity in cross-examination, masterful logic, corroding satire, a deadly suavity, wonderful skill in suggestion.

Then suddenly the briefs are shot back at the attorneys; Sir Edward will not come into court at any figure; he has greater work on hand : there is an Ulster Government to be formed, an Ulster Army to be raised and drilled, guns to be "run," laws to be broken. Once, indeed, the great man relented and put on his wig—to represent a member of that Government which he was defying and denouncing. On the strength of such piquant incidents in the life of a Frondist, there are those who hold that all that complicated business of the Ulster Force and the Provisional Government was a gigantic bluff. Who knows? True, it is not usual for a real rebel to have a house in Eaton Place and a week-end cottage at Rottingdean, to insist on a fire in his bathroom, and to remain "the most popular man in the House of Commons" by virtue of his social gifts. But nature is rich, and one anomaly the more means little to her.

Perhaps it is better frankly to give up as hopeless the attempt to discover what Sir Edward Carson really is, and devote ourselves to the simpler problem of defining what he is not. We now know that he is not a statesman. He is as little a statesman as Sir Frederick Smith. The rather vague hopes built on the fact that he could speak well (if rather confusedly),

that he was rich, and that he was excessively pug-
nacious, are now seen to have been entirely fallacious.
Sir Edward Carson has been many things. He was
an excellent tomahawk in the hands of others. He has
shown, like Parnell and Lenin, a certain power of
destructive organization. He has even filled routine
posts with fair credit. But of the higher statesmanship of creation, or even the lower statesmanship of
imaginative administration, he has indicated no trace.
His mind is, indeed, only strong on the negative side.
Even in advocacy he always relied rather on breaking
an adversary's case than on developing his own.
" My lord, I must object," is his attitude to everything. He objects to Prussia, as he did to Home Rule.
But he has no positive formula with which to confront
Prussianism, any more than he had a positive pro-
gramme to confront Home Rulers.

Indeed, it would be hard for him to evolve one, for
he is himself not a little touched with the infertile
spirit of Prussia. So personally amiable a man could
not, of course, have anything but loathing for the
grosser abominations of Potsdam. He has none of
the Junker's blood-lust, and none of his griping
avarice. But he is cursed with not a little of the
Prussian sterility. His mind has the harshness of the
east wind of the Baltic flats and the gritty unfriendli-
ness of the soil of Mecklenburg. It is destitute of
sympathy, of insight, of flexibility. His head is hard,
with the hardness of iron-wood, which is still wood.

Within its narrow limits the Carson intellect is as
keen as the razor-like Carson face. But nothing will
grow on a razor except the rust that spoils it. Even
in his own profession Sir Edward Carson has produced
little but verdicts and vast fees. He does not belong
to the Mansfields and Eldons. No eager student at
the Temple will ever turn to him for illuminating
exposition of that enormous legend of the law. Only
those who aim to be masters of the art of browbeating

will study with emulous admiration the classics of cross-examination which lie to his credit.

In some respects the Prussian has an advantage over Sir Edward. He, at least, knows Europe, though with the lower knowledge of hate; Sir Edward does not even know England, perhaps not Ireland. The Prussian has some wooden sense of construction, though we may chiefly pray to be saved from what he builds : Sir Edward Carson has only made name and fame as a critic or a destroyer. The Prussian aims at a soulless kind of symmetry : Sir Edward strives for the perpetuation of the amorphous. He is rightly insistent on the satisfaction of the French claim for Alsace-Lorraine. Yet his attitude to the Irish of his own native Dublin is-that of the Prussian garrison in Alsace. He regards them with the stiff Prussian intolerance for a happier and perhaps healthier race.

The whole truth about the Ulster intrigues will probably not emerge in our lifetimes. Whether the fanatic or the party man was uppermost when Sir Edward Carson blessed the Covenant of contingent rebellion in the presence of the Ulster lords and Galloper Smith—this we do not and cannot know. But we do know now—Mr. Gerard has made it clear— that Potsdam betted heavily on Carsonism. Potsdam may have been wrong. But some part of the readiness with which Germany accepted a great risk was un- doubtedly due to the conviction that the schism was real and serious, that it affected the discipline of the British Army, and would probably paralyze British diplomacy.

In the general truce and amnesty of 1914 these things were more or less forgotten in England. Un- happily they could not be forgotten in Ireland. When the Coalition of 1915 was formed, Mr. Redmond stood out; Sir Edward Carson came in; and with his entry, conveying the implication that Home Rule was dead, went the last hope of maintaining Irish unity, already

impaired by War Office mistakes. The only apparent
explanation of this great political blunder was that
"Ulster's strong man" would be safer inside the
Cabinet than out. But Mr. Asquith lost Ireland without even gaining Sir Edward Carson. In a few months
he flung out of the Cabinet in a pet, and became the
centre of a new set of disintegrating intrigues.

His reputation gained enormously by a dramatic
revolt against supposed incompetence, and there were
millions who hailed him as chief Sandow when Mr.
Lloyd George formed his Cabinet of strong and silent
men. But Sir Edward Carson was fated not to satisfy
these expectations. That force of character which
had prevailed against the British Cabinet and the
Irish Government was powerless against the German
submarine and the Admiralty "dug-out." It was
understood that the Carson broom was to make a
clean sweep of all the cobwebs which had collected
under Mr. Balfour's gentle sway. It may have been
all a myth; there may have been no cobwebs. In any
case Sir Edward Carson's advent made no perceptible
difference. He announced betimes that he knew
nothing of naval affairs and should be guided in all
things by his advisers; that pledge he seems to have
fulfilled to the letter. Before, however, he had well
settled down the Prime Minister decided on placing
Sir Eric Geddes, the ex-railway manager, in his place,
and it was announced that Sir Edward Carson's calm
wisdom would now be unrestrictedly at the disposal
of the War Cabinet.

Shortly it appeared exactly how the calm wisdom
was to be employed. Propaganda, it seemed, was
needed to bring home to the British masses the justice
of the cause for which this country had been fighting
for over three years. It had to be explained that our
sword was drawn in the interests of small nationalities,
for the vindication of public law, and for the further-
ance of democratic ideals. It might be thought that

this quite measurable task could have been entrusted to a statesman of less questionable eminence—one who had never employed a private commander-in-chief, landed guns for contingent rebellion, or obtained conditional promises from " some of the greatest generals in the Army." Yet Sir Edward Carson was chosen to convince the British Pacifist of his errors. It was a grim and costly jest on Mr. Asquith's part to entrust him, as Attorney-General, with the guardianship of laws he had boasted of breaking. It was an even subtler pleasantry to make him the chief director of our spiritual munition department.

Sir Edward Carson is troubled, however, with no inconvenient sense of humour, and stolidly carried out his duties despite the toning down of his "Talk to me of a League of Nations" speech, and other rather embarrassing outbursts. But the re-emergence of the Irish question at last brought matters to a head. It became plain that Sir Edward could no longer serve the King and "Ulster" at one and the same time. He chose Ulster, and resigned for the second time in three years. It might have been thought that at last his mind was made up to confine himself to Irish affairs. But his political ambitions, despite the contempt he always expresses for politics, are believed to be too importunate for comfort in the cold shades. There is already talk of new combinations. It is suggested that Sir Edward is more than a little interested in the so-called "National" Party, chiefly consisting of dissatisfied Unionists. But it may well be questioned whether this singular man, the strangest fanatic the present generation has seen, will ever lead any considerable body of Englishmen.

For Sir Edward Carson has no quality that appeals to the English except his undoubted courage. His solemn rants are not understood by a people prone to under-expression of their deeper feelings. Even in 1914 his heroics, like the speeches of the German

Emperor, savoured faintly of ridicule. Now they seem quite unpleasantly out of harmony with the general mood. Mere verbal intemperance, however, is often treated by the English with strange tolerance. It is levity in action which arouses the deep and lasting distrust of the masses of this country. Lord Randolph Churchill was considered to have stuff in him until he resigned; after that, though he often talked more wisely than before, he had no audience.

Sir Edward Carson lost any popular following he might have had in Great Britain when his second resignation was published. What hold he may retain on individual Unionist statesmen is less easy to determine; it is whispered that nobody is precisely anxious to co-operate with him again. But Irish miseries acquaint politicians with strange bedfellows, and while it is impossible to get on with Sir Edward it may well prove equally impossible to get on without him.

MR. ASQUITH

There are certain things that England does very well, and Mr. Asquith is one of them. One may quarrel with the stuff and the fashion; but given material and mode of treatment, malice itself cannot deny that the product in its own way is very perfect.

If one had to express this eminent man in terms of chemistry, the chief symbols would stand for his native Yorkshire town and for Balliol and its famous master, that rather cynical instructor of budding statesmen, Dr. Jowett. Mr. Asquith may be called the Jowettate of Middleclassdom. The base of the compound is of course his own sterling English intelligence, weighty and acute, but rather prosaic; but its character has been profoundly modified by the culture of Oxford.

Herbert Henry Asquith was born in 1852 at Morley, and almost his earliest recollection is of walking as a Sunday-school child in a local procession to celebrate the Crimean peace. Morley is one of those smaller towns of the West Riding which, while closely connected with the great seats of the staple industries, remain free from the cosmopolitan atmosphere of Leeds and Bradford, and conserve a strongly developed local consciousness. A town of little graciousness of aspect, rather overweighted architecturally with Nonconformist chapels, it is hardly a spot to which the weary man of the world, *qui mores hominum multorum vidit et urbes,* returns lovingly in his old age. But there are many worse places a clever and ambitious youth of the middling class might choose to be born in. The village and the country town tend to stagnation; in great centres youth is apt to be stunned by the vastness of everything : the seeming futility of a duel between the immature individual and his environment has no doubt crushed many a young Londoner of good natural parts. A place like Morley, itself quite measurable, but in no sense shut in, was capable at once of dissatisfying and stimulating. There was little to encourage passivity where the horizon was the chief interest. Of Morley, with its breadth and narrowness, its hard common sense and rather raw materialism, there is still a good deal in Mr. Asquith. With all his culture there remains much of the middle-class mind, with its good and its not so good. Despite an excellent acquaintance with literature, and a generally good taste therein, he is in many matters something of a Philistine. He belongs distinctly to the Victorians, and would be wholly at home in Gath and Askelon. In political tendencies as in literary tastes he is old-fashioned. Fate has mixed him up with the social reformers, but his heart has never been with them ; it beats constant to Stuart Mill. Perhaps here

again Morley helps; the statesman remembers certain
realities noted by the middle-class youth; and that
recollection forbids any illusion as to the sudden per-
fectibility of the working masses, or, for that matter,
of their masters. Mr. Asquith is no democrat. But
he is very sincerely a Liberal of the old individualist
philosophy, and therefore a real and sane thing, if a
limited one. His Nonconformist ancestry is little
visible in externals; no man likes better the theatre,
cards, the chatter of attractive women, or the consola-
tions of good fiction. But there is nevertheless in the
grain of him a good deal of the Puritan, old and new;
the old came out in his obstinate duel with the Peerage,
the new (more soft-hearted and less hard-headed) was
shown in his incapacity to understand the real Prussia.

It is tempting to speculate how the mind and character of Mr. Asquith would have reacted to circumstances such as those of Mr. Lloyd George's boyhood.
Would they have mellowed or embittered, widened or
narrowed, made him more or less human? How much
has Mr. Asquith or the British world gained or lost
by the circumstance that life was made smooth, but
not too smooth, for him? "I can't have your advantages, and you can't have mine," wrote the self-made
American to his son. "One man learns the value of
truth by going to Sunday School and another by
doing business with liars. One man is sober because
he had a good mother, and another because his father
drank the boots off his feet." If Mr. Asquith was
destitute of Mr. Lloyd George's peculiar educational
advantages he enjoyed many of a different kind, and
made the most of them. At the City of London
School he captured all the prizes; at Oxford he became
President of the Union, took the highest degrees,
carried off the Craven Scholarship, made the right
kind of friends. Jowett was rightly proud of him.
"Asquith is the one pupil of mine," he said, "for
whom I can most confidently predict success in life."

" Asquith will get on," he said, on another occasion,
" he is so direct." Jowettery was the philosophy of
getting on in its most dignified guise, a sublimated
opportunism, in which worship of the main chance
was robbed of its grossness and made a fit faith for a
scholar and a gentleman.

Jowett was justified of his spiritual child. Young
Asquith did get on, and by "direct" means. Apart
from the paternal means which assured him a first-
rate education, no man of our time owes less to external
help or more to his own abilities. The Bar, with
Westminster in the offing, naturally attracted him.
At a very early age he had confided to a friend his
ambition—either to be Lord Chancellor or Prime
Minister—and the Bar was his only road to the Woolsack of the Treasury. The capacity of getting at facts
and stating them with the utmost lucidity was Mr.
Asquith's from boyhood. Certain pleadings, drawn
by an unknown junior, attracted the attention of a
great lawyer by their grasp and clearness; and from
that moment the professional success of the young
aspirant was assured. A wider reputation was achieved
by his appearance before the Parnell Commission; and
this had hardly been confirmed before Mr. Gladstone,
struck by the quality of his first Parliamentary speech,
offered him the great post of Home Secretary. There
were many who saw rashness in the experiment; but
such doubts could not long survive; in his first official
job Mr. Asquith acquitted himself as if years of experience were behind him; he spoke like a wise old
man and acted like a young and courageous one. Yet,
despite this precocious success, he hardly impressed
his contemporaries as a future Prime Minister. It was
not then quite so emphatically as now the day of the
lawyer-politician; the Woolsack rather than Downing
Street was the normal goal of a barrister M.P. To
people soaked in the Gladstonian tradition, too, the
coldness of Mr. Asquith's temperament, reflected in a

most austere diction, seemed to disqualify him for a
party leader. The hardness of youth has since been
somewhat toned down; advancing years have given
rather more warmth and humanity to Mr. Asquith's
periods. But his then style of speaking, though of
great merit, was somewhat too bare and bloodless to
delight a generation accustomed to the Victorian grand
manner. A better description could not be than that
of Mr. Asquith's present wife when she was still Miss
Tennant and a comparative stranger : "He has a very
good voice and the rare qualities that make a great
speaker—imagination, restraint, brevity, and *l'oreille
juste*. He does not strain the attention by discursive
parentheses, and is neither too precious, too pedantic,
nor too prepared to be listened to with confidence and
pleasure."

Higher praise in its kind could not be given; but
this style of speaking was hardly even caviare to the
select of those days. But there was probably a deeper
reason for the failure to recognize in the young Home
Secretary something more than the ordinary careerist
lawyer. Mr. Asquith has at no time given the impression of all that is in him. He does not advertise.
He has never cultivated the Press. He has made no
obeisance to the mob, even to the mob called society.
He disdains all kinds of display, and habitually under-
states his personality. Moreover, he exercises a
curious economy of effort, almost amounting to
miserliness. There are some statesmen who give the
impression of being indefinably above their best in
performance; there are others who occasion a constant
surprise, not that they fail to acquit themselves well,
but that they are able to carry out their functions at
all. Mr. Balfour is the great living representative of
the former type. A net cast at random anywhere in
Whitehall would secure a specimen of the latter. Mr.
Asquith occupies an almost unique position between
these extremes. He has never, like Mr. Balfour, sug-

gested a vague and even disappointing superiority,
making one feel that the result is less than it ought to
be : he generally appears adequate, and a little more,
to the particular task in hand, while somehow failing
to give the idea of supreme power. One might summarize by saying that he has strength without mystery.
He shows an easy mastery, an almost careless compe-
tence, as that of an express locomotive which always
has a little "in hand" even on its fastest run. Its
steady mechanical puff contrasts with the laboured
panting of some little shunting engine; it does its
regular fifty miles an hour, rises now and again to
seventy, and might do a hundred for all one knows.
But there is no witchery in the business, except perhaps to a savage; indeed, it is rather the other way :
the splendour of the performance is obscured by its
very ease.

Thus it was that, even in his Liberal Imperialist
days, Mr. Asquith was counted second to a brilliant
trifler like Lord Rosebery; that it was considered quite
natural that he should serve under a mediocrity like
Sir Henry Campbell-Bannerman; and rather un-
natural that on the death of the latter King Edward
should send for him as the only obvious Prime
Minister. Mr. Lloyd George and Mr. Churchill were
far more in the public eye; Mr. Haldane had achieved
a success apparently as solid and rather more picturesque; Sir Edward Grey enjoyed a perhaps larger
prestige.

As Chancellor of the Exchequer—after all only his
second official post—Mr. Asquith had shown himself
competent, but hardly inspired; the merit of Old Age
Pensions, which he had provided for, was claimed
by others; and the memory of the services he had
rendered to the Liberal Party by his great speeches
in the Tariff controversy seemed scarcely more recent
to the Radical stalwarts than the (to them) less
fragrant recollections of his "Tabernacle" and

" Clean Slate " days.   The Liberal Party had had
one bitter experience of a leader out of touch with the
rank-and-file of the party ; there were very many who
believed Mr. Asquith would prove as disastrous a
liability as Lord Rosebery.   A year or two later the
same men were comparing him, with good intentions
but real unkindness, to Cromwell, in their laudation
of his victory over the House of Lords.

On the merits of that great conflict nothing need be
said.   But as a mere exhibition of tenacity, tactical
skill, and patient courage the fight that followed the
Lords' rejection of the Budget of 1909 was remarkable.
Mr. Asquith not only inflicted defeat ; he made
recovery impossible.   He was, of course, helped by
the mistakes of the enemy ; Lord Lansdowne might
explain away his final surrender as a submission to
force majeure, but he had already given away the
moral case by his own Reform proposals.   The House
of Lords emerged from the struggle not only worsted,
but a self-confessed anachronism, an admittedly class
institution, composed for the most part of men whom
its leader had deliberately described as unfit to dis-
charge the functions of a Second Chamber.   It had,
moreover, been placed in the invidious position of at
least seeming to prefer the trumpery of titles, dignities,
ribands, and social prestige to real power and dignity
in the State.   Nor was it the least bitter part of the
whole business that in the long conflict moderation,
restraint, and legalistic propriety were on the side
of the Prime Minister, while revolutionary froth,
violence, and lawlessness were the badge of the
defenders of privilege.

The conduct of this campaign established Mr.
Asquith's reputation as a great master of Parliamentary craft.   The sequel was to reveal his weaker
side.   The Unionist leaders, manœuvred into a false
position, twice defeated at the polls, faced with schism
over the belated submission to threats of a swamping

creation of peers, played their last desperate card.
They produced from their sleeves the Ulster trump,
the Knave of anarchy, and Mr. Asquith would not or
could not play the King of lawful authority. He decided
only to wait and see, and did actually see at the last
what he should have foreseen from the first. The
reputation which had been impaired by a practical
breakdown of government in the spring and summer
of 1914 was partially restored during the first months
of the war. Mr. Asquith then emerged, if not as a
great war Minister, at least as the splendid spokesman
of the nation. He is often sneered at as a mere
lawyer. But it was the lawyer's horror of Prussian
lawlessness that moved the man so tremendously as
to give his earlier war speeches the moral fervour of
a crusade as well as the balance and precision of a
statesman. Mr. Asquith's words at this time were of
almost incalculable worth to the Allies in a world still
largely neutral, by no means unfriendly to Germany
on general grounds, and keenly critical of all kinds of
pretensions. A mishandling of our case might have
had the gravest effects; it was, in fact, handled with
supreme skill.

Administration was also characterized by great
energy and judgment. With marvellous smoothness,
considering the tremendous blow delivered to the
habits and prepossessions of centuries, the transition
was made from a state of profound peace to a state of
war on every ocean and in almost every continent.
Mr. Asquith has been assailed both for our unpre-
paredness for war, and for the delay with which, after
the actual declaration, our latent resources were made
available. The fuller knowledge of another generation
will probably render an entirely different verdict. It
will lay stress on the speed with which moderate
existing means were mobilized, on the astonishing
efficiency of their employment, and on the wide scope
and vigorous nature of the measures taken for the

ultimate increase of Great Britain's contribution.
Whether this enormous energy could in any case have
been maintained is a question that cannot be resolved.
It is scarcely doubtful that it was not maintained.
The formation of the First Coalition Government may
have proceeded from Mr. Asquith's conviction that
new blood was necessary, or it may have been forced
on him by quite different considerations; but in any
case the fall of the Liberal Administration was a
practical confession of failure somewhere or somehow.

In some respects the record of the reconstructed
Government was even more melancholy than that of
its predecessor. For rapidly multiplying resources
were more than nullified by multiplying reverses and
misfortunes. The gloomy years 1915 and 1916 could
show little to the credit of an account which displayed
on its debit side the disappointments of Gallipoli and
Mesopotamia, the great and immediately unfruitful
expenditure of life on the Western front, the Russian
reverses, the overrunning of Serbia and Rumania,
the losses by submarine, the unchecked aerial in-
vasions, and the Irish rebellion. How far Mr.
Asquith, as head of the Administration, could be
justly held responsible for military and diplomatic
failures is a question not to be lightly answered;
while it would be unjust to ignore the skill with which
he reconciled the nation to conscription and Labour
to the modification of trade union practice. But,
when every allowance is made, both for the inherent
difficulties of the exterior situation and for constant
Cabinet and Parliamentary intrigues which embarrassed and finally overthrew him, it may well be that
there will remain something unrebutted in the general
indictment of Mr. Asquith as a war Minister.

Indeed, there are features of his character and
general habit of mind which would largely explain
such failure. Though he prefers to give the world an
impression of coldness, he is really a most kindly man,

in whom loyalty to friends and the desire to "get on"
are dangerously prone to affect judgment. Macaulay
has remarked that the worst of all rulers is he who
puts the feelings of those he sees daily before the
interests of the millions he will never see and who
will sacrifice a distant province in order to be surrounded by smiling faces. Mr. Asquith, who has been
described as " the comrade rather than the chief " of
his fellow-Ministers, would no doubt not consciously
neglect a public duty on account of a private partiality.
But in fact his policy often suffered because it pained
him to throw over a friend or irked him to put his foot
down on a rebel. It was so in peace, and it has been
so in war. A wise regard for " national unity " has,
it may be suspected, sometimes been reinforced by
disinclination to be disagreeable. Moreover, he is an
easy man in another sense. The word "indolent"
might be more accurately used but for the fact that it
is so little understood how much of the best work of
the world is done by indolent people. Mr. Asquith
possesses immense reserves of mental energy, but, like
many millionaires, he likes to keep a large balance and
has an objection to drawing cheques. He can get
through the work of half a dozen men when pressed,
but he prefers to economize effort when possible. This
tendency has been the main cause of the many em-
barrassments in which he has been involved. Again
and again, before the war, it looked as if the Government must fall, when Mr. Asquith has put matters
right by a masterpiece of legerdemain. But this very
skill in saving desperate situations, and loosing the
most fearsome tangle " familiar as his garter," only
proves the existence of a weakness. The finest driver
may be unfortunate sometimes, and when an accident
happens to his team it goes to his credit that he has
made the best of a bad job. But the man whose horses
are always going down on their knees will not be
chosen as a Royal whip, though he possesses a very

genius for getting them on their legs again without serious damage. The plain man takes the view that the best coachman is he who needs such dexterity least. Mr. Asquith showed great resource, for example, in dealing with the miserable Curragh affair. A less dexterous Minister would have been ruined. But many Ministers of quite moderate capacity would have avoided the trouble altogether.

This lack of vigilance is partly, no doubt, due to the lawyer's habit of leaving things till they arise. It is the only way for a barrister in large practice. The advocate who has to prosecute a forger on Monday, to defend an interesting murderer on Tuesday, and to lead in a sensational libel action on Wednesday week, will concentrate his mind on the first before he even begins to think about the others; he knows nothing will happen in the meanwhile : the interesting murderer will not be hanged before he has disposed of the forger, and nothing will happen without notice in the libel case. In the realm of action, however, nothing can be left unwatched; the price of safety is perpetual vigilance. Yet the habits of a lifetime are apt to govern the lawyer-statesman, and he often tends to make his power of rapidly grasping a situation when it arises the excuse for not foreseeing and providing for it in advance. The fault, it may be observed, is by no means confined to statesmen belonging to the higher branch of the profession.

But if it may reasonably be contended that Mr. Asquith has most real defects as a chief Minister, and that those defects were reflected in his war administration, common gratitude should have recognized the great value of his contribution to the common stock, and common decency should have prevented the base outcry against him when he left office. The cold magnanimity with which he has passed over much public injustice and much private treachery is a quality peculiar to him. Few men have been attacked with

more virulence; he is almost alone in never replying
to such attacks. Yet his forbearance does not conciliate, and is probably not meant to do so. There is,
indeed, something enormously insulting in his professed indifference—professed only, for he is at bottom
a sensitive man and feels keenly wounds he disdains
to betray by a wince or a whimper or a retort. He will
go to immense pains to defend a colleague when the
colleague is in the right, and often when he is in the
wrong; but when he himself is concerned slander goes
unanswered. Like William III., when asked why he
did not notice a foul libel, he would doubtless say,
" J'ai pensé que c'était au dessous de moi."

Few politicians, too, can boast so complete an
immunity from any form of untruth. There have
been times when it seemed impossible to believe that
Mr. Asquith was stating the facts, yet circumstances
have always established his absolute veracity in spirit
and in letter. It is, indeed, little short of marvellous
that he is so seldom betrayed into unconscious inac-
curacies. But his principles are fixed, if he shows
some squeezability in detail; he has really what is
rare enough to-day, a political philosophy. Few men
more consistently refer to first principles in dealing
with problems of the moment; and, knowing himself
how to reason, it is easy to understand that he has
some contempt for those who know only how to declaim. His memory is extraordinary; his intellect is
always under control; and his language, though
precise, is guarded. It is probably little known how
much care often goes to the composition of utterances
which fill the discerning critics with despairing admiration. Mr. Asquith can, indeed, speak well without
any kind of preparation. His mentality is so disciplined, and his instinct for the right word is so infallible, that his impromptus are scarcely less clear-cut
in their bronze massiveness than his more elaborate
efforts. But when he is engaged on a speech or a

document which he regards as vitally important no pains are too great; he will go over the whole thing, line by line and word by word, submit and resubmit it to criticism, and part with it only when he is assured that it cannot be bettered.   In preparing statements meant for American reading, for example, he is infinitely careful not to employ any expression, however correct according to our usage, which might have a different shade of meaning on the other side of the Atlantic.

But, after all, Mr. Asquith is a wholly truthful man, chiefly because he is also, with all his limitation, a wholly true man.   Behind his intellectual accomplishment is a character that extorts respect from all who are themselves worthy of being respected. He is not least English in his complete honesty. The machine of his mind may not be fitted for some work, but it is true and well wrought. His character may lack some of the graces, but its foundations are as adamant. The victim of much small meanness is himself incapable of anything small or mean. Opinions may vary widely as to Mr. Asquith's political game. But the candid observer must admit that he has always played it like a gentleman.

THE EARL OF DERBY

Lord Derby is not the sort of man of whom one would wish to speak flippantly. He is entitled to the same sort of respect one pays to a fifteenth-century manor house now used as a tavern. It bears witness to a venerable past. It enjoys a comfortable and useful present. Lord Derby has the same double claim on our regard. As a monument he is more interesting than the Albert Memorial. As a human individual he is not destitute of a certain modest merit. He has censored Press telegrams, convicted poachers, done a little soldiering of the ornamental kind, gone through the motions of controlling the Post Office (the real workers have not forgotten that he called them a set of "bloodsuckers"), and done most of the things a great noble is supposed to do. And there is much health in him.

His earlier war service now belongs to history, and we will let history deal with it. He carried through the voluntary recruiting campaign with much bustle and hustle, and rounded it off with probably the most confused statement ever published as an official paper. Still, the thing was done. As Under-Secretary for the War Office in Lord Kitchener's time, he was not conspicuously wanting; he knew something about the Department, and he was not the man to stray far from the beaten track. No doubt Lord Derby has all kinds of virtues in a subordinate position. He might even go unchallenged as a chief in times when it is clearly understood that public work matters little, and party claims matter much. Unfortunately, these times are wholly different. It does matter who controls the War Office during the greatest war of history; and when Lord Derby assumed that control his inadequacy was too obvious to be obscured by any irrelevant prestige.

If blue blood supplied the place of grey matter, and the intricacies of a family tree were as important as the convolutions of a living brain, Lord Derby need have feared no criticism. He has almost too much blue blood. It deepens the ruddiness of his pleasant face, and even gives him rather the effect of wearing too tight a collar. No living man can claim more. On his mother's side he descends from the Clarendons, and he is the seventeenth Stanley to sign himself "Derby." One of his ancestors was that Lord Stanley who betrayed Richard III. at Bosworth, and earned the favour of the unkingly Richmond.

Another sat in judgment on Mary, Queen of Scots.
The Derbys enjoyed regal powers in the Isle of Man,
and one of the race refused the throne of Greece
some time last century, preferring, in Disraeli's bom-
bastic phrase, Knowsley to the Parthenon and Lancashire to the Attic Plains.

In personal honours and endowments, Lord Derby
is equally fortunate. His ancestors, common-sense
men who kept steadily on the right side in politics,
have handed down to him title-deeds to seventy thousand acres, including the site of a good deal of Liver-
pool. He is a Knight of the Garter. For better or
worse he is also a Knight of Grace of St. John of
Jerusalem and a member of the Jockey Club. And
he is a fine large man, who looks extremely well in
his robes; perhaps a little less well in the ordinary
dress of a well-to-do Englishman, for all the skill of
his tailor does not hide the fact that there is just a
little too much of him.

If you should happen to meet Lord Derby, knowing who he was, you could hardly fail to think him
a very remarkable man. You would revel in his fine
bluff English manner. You would find a subtle charm
in the way in which, as his admirers note, he " calls
a spade a spade." The blunt features, the full neck,
the shrewd eyes, and unfurrowed forehead would all
become significant. For it is not in human nature—
certainly not in British nature—to separate the man
from his title, his acres, his pedigree, and the fuss and
prestige of it all.

But if you were to meet Lord Derby in a first-class
carriage going North, you would probably get the
impression of a prosperous manufacturer blossoming
into a Park Laner. He has just a suspicion of the
Lancashire accent, and more than a touch of the Lancashire brusqueness. He radiates, too, the strong but
limited common sense of the type.

Again, if you transferred his Lordship from first

class to third, took off his Jermyn Street kit and clothed him in cheap tweeds, you might just as easily take him for a trade union delegate. I remember, indeed, seeing him pointed out, on an occasion when Ministers were on show, as one of the Labour Members, whereas Mr. George Barnes was unconsciously masquerading as a member of the hereditary aristocracy. Indeed, Lord Derby, had some night-tripping fairy changed him at birth, might with no great incongruity fill the part of secretary to the Amalgamated Society of Brewery and Aerated Water Trades Transport Workers.

He has something of the Tudor roughness. Like Harry the Eighth, one can well imagine him wrestling with a butcher on a village green, and kissing the butcher's sweetheart after giving him his licking. He is equally at home with the masses and the classes. He is not only a man of the world but a man of more worlds than one. The shades of sixteen Earls of the Stanley blood do not prevent him from descending, on selected occasions, to demagogy. He is at home with a comedian in the green-room, a bookmaker on the turf, or an interrupter at a public meeting. If the late George Wyndham might be taken as the Athos of British aristocracy, and Lord Lansdowne as its Aramis, Lord Derby is even more its Porthos. So rich, so insolently brave, with so much muscle, and—well, Porthos needs no further description.

But Porthos had, with all his bluffness, an occasional weakness for the part of Aramis. He sometimes intrigued—though not in the manner of M. l'Abbé. Now intrigue is exactly what Lord Derby cannot abide. "We'll have no intriguers here!" he has said in the decisive tones of Mistress Quickly on "swaggerers." The mere facts are, of course, that in the transactions that led to Mr. Asquith's resignation Lord Derby played a not unimportant part. He —supported Mr. Lloyd George militant, and received his reward from Mr. Lloyd George triumphant. But was there here any intrigue? Let Lord Derby himself answer. In the course of a handsome eulogium on himself, delivered a few days after the change of Government, he remarked : " I know of no intrigues. I would not have been in one if I had known it, you may rest assured." And, as if this were not enough, he returned to the subject ten minutes later. " I hope you will believe that I will never be disloyal, and I will never enter into an intrigue." He had, he said, " no personal motive of any sort or kind," " no ulterior motive whatever " : there never was such a categorical negative since the Grand Inquisitor's in *The Gondoliers.*

Of course, one takes the noble Earl's word for it. But one cannot help feeling rather like Mr. Micawber after his wife has assured him for the sixtieth time that she would never desert him : " My dear, I am not conscious that you are expected to do anything of the sort." It needed no such emphasis to make us believe Lord Derby; indeed, such is the inconsistency of human nature, we might have had a somewhat more profound sense of his disinterestedness had he less insisted on calling attention to it. Nobody thinks Lord Derby self-seeking in the vulgar sense. Men with seventy thousand rich acres are seldom that. Becky Sharp has put it on record that she would have been an innocent lamb on fifty thousand a year. There are, however, other objects of ambition beside the salary of a Minister.

At any rate, though he does not intrigue, Lord Derby is by no means indifferent to things which sometimes interest intriguers. He knows how to manage an editor just as well as an audience. Perhaps Mr. Lloyd George told him all about it. He fully understands what is meant by a good Press. He is even suspected of deliberately adopting the John Bull pose—as deliberately as Mr. Bottomley, whom he

rather resembles in Bullish frankness and sturdy indiscretion. Unlike Mr. Balfour, he diligently reads
the papers, and is not altogether displeased when they
comment on his upright and downright slap-a-man-on-
the-shoulder heartiness. It was perhaps not quite an
accident that the idea of a Centre Party began to gain
ground just after his elevation, though it was, of
course, pure chance that "a level-headed, patriotic,
practical, all-British and no-nonsense statesman—Lord
Derby is the type of man who springs to the eye "—
was immediately suggested as the Centre Party's
chief.

Lord Derby's newspaper reputation stood him in
good stead during a year of great office. He might not
be brilliant, but who wants brilliance in England?
He might not be very apprehensive or sympathetic,
but Holdfast and Grumble are the dogs for many
Britons' money. Lord Derby had two qualities that
rendered others unnecessary. He was English, and
he was Straight. A more rectilinear politician could
not be. The malignant critic might point to verbal
inconsistencies. He might show an unkept promise
here, an unfulfilled calculation there, an indefensible
piece of red-tape somewhere else. That was the
system. It could not be Lord Derby, the moral
parallelogram of the British peerage.

But at last people began to ask why Lord Derby
should be at the War Office at all, if the " system "
ran itself. Murmurs began to be heard, and presently
swelled into a considerable volume of straight speech.
It became the fashion to talk of the "soullessness "
of the War Office. Lord Derby, it seems, had been
expected to radiate soul in Whitehall. More substantial critics suggested that the Department had
by no means kept pace with the increasing demands
on its intelligence and resource. For some time this
flood of censure was, as usual, pooh-poohed in public
and anxiously discussed in private. Mr. Lloyd George,

always quick to distinguish between criticism with
and criticism without a popular backing, was not long
in deciding that a change was necessary.

The manner of the change was highly characteristic.
The Prime Minister satisfied at once his instinct for
the safe course and his relish for a practical jest. He
made Lord Milner Secretary for War and Lord Derby
Ambassador in Paris. The French are said to be
delighted. The English were amused, and not displeased. The voice of criticism was silenced. Am-
bassadors, like Kings, cannot be exposed to common
censure.

VISCOUNT GREY OF FALLODON

VISCOUNT GREY—he prefers the more formal style to
avoid confusion with other lordly Greys—is, or was,
known in Germany as "Liar Grey." To Germans,
in their present haste, all Englishmen are liars. But
this Englishman is prince and chief of liars. He
stands on a lonely pinnacle. His home is in the higher
Alps of mendacity, far above the line of stunted truth
and the edelweiss of small deceit, in the region of
eternal falsity.

It is a curious example of the mirage effects of an
atmosphere of war and hate. In this country Viscount
Grey has many critics and possibly a few enemies.
He has been attacked as a reckless Imperialist and
derided as a futile and bewildered Pacifist. There are
some who think that he might have avoided war by
concession, and more who think that he might at least
have postponed it by boldness. He is an object of
real mistrust to a section of his own party, and of
affected contempt to those who denounce what they
call the "Old Gang." In the reaction against a once
common idolatry there are many who suggest that his

solemnity was only the mask of puzzle-headed mediocrity. More rationally it is held that no man was ever
so wise as Viscount Grey looked, and that no small
part of his great prestige was due to his Roman profile,
his aloof manner, and his rigid economy in speech.

Viscount Grey, indeed, has been, since his resignation, a target for all the shafts that go the way of the
wounded buck. But nobody in this country has yet
cast an imputation on his veracity. There are some
accusations that malice itself rejects. Mr. Bernard
Shaw's bitterest enemy never accused him of Vitellian
gluttony. The Archbishop of Canterbury has escaped
denunciation as a fanatic. It is rarely suggested that
Mr. Belloc's great-grandfather was a rabbi, or that
Mr. Chesterton draws his main income from an illicit
cocoa factory. So with Viscount Grey. Nobody
accuses him of lying for the same reason that nobody
compliments him on telling the truth; it would be
simply silly to do so.

That is the common view among Englishmen. If it
be objected that we are partial the answer is " Call
Prince Lichnowsky." The late German Ambassador
watched the late Foreign Secretary, during many
critical months, with close and suspicious scrutiny.
He had, of all men, motive and opportunity to apply
the severest tests. Writing in retirement, far from
any associations likely to disturb his judgment, he has
set down in a document intended only for posterity
his deliberate judgment of the man his countrymen
denounce especially as a liar. " The simplicity and
honesty of his ways," says the Prince, " secured him
the esteem even of his opponents. Lies and intrigue
were equally repugnant to him."

How then are we to account for the fact that, while
Mr. Asquith and others are attacked on various
grounds, the consistent German charge against
Viscount Grey is that so coarsely conveyed in the
epithet applied to him? In all German outbursts one

constant note is struck with evident sincerity. We
are the "treacherous" English. The Germans clearly
believe the expectations they formed concerning our
attitude to be rationally founded : hence their rage
against the man who misled them. The truth, it may
be guessed, can be expressed in the reversal of a
famous epigram. "Il ment toujours; il ne trompe
jamais," said Talleyrand of a Teutonic statesman.
Sir Edward Grey never lied, but he did deceive. It
was not his fault, of course. He told the simple truth
on every occasion, expecting himself to be understood
as doing so. German statesmen, accustomed to weigh
every possibility but this, always read into his words
more or less than their face value, which happened to
be also their real value.

In 1913 Viscount Grey's policy was generally
applauded in this country as not only generous but
wise. In many quarters it is now conceived to have
been less wise than generous. But it was always
perfectly consistent and straightforward. He clung
to the understanding with France, of which Mr.
Balfour's prescient wisdom had seen the necessity.
He extended that understanding to Russia. But
while maintaining these friendships, he sought to
remove all causes of friction with Germany, as a
preliminary to establishing better relations all round
and placing the peace of Europe on a stable basis.

We know now that it was all a dream. But there
are some who still believe, despite a mass of evidence
to the contrary, that it was a dream not only capable
of realization, but very nearly realized. No doubt
Viscount Grey, perhaps misled by the enthusiasm of
Lord Haldane, gravely miscalculated the forces in
Germany making for war. It is pretty certain that,
when the feeble German peace party was overwhelmed,
every honest attempt on his part to reach an accommodation only made matters worse. *Sous*-Bismarcks
of the Kiderlen-Waechter stamp, Pan-Germans *en-*

ragés like Tirpitz, only interpreted his bids for German friendship as half-promises to betray France and Russia on suitable terms. Every approach was mis-read. Plain statements were invested with sinister significance. There are, indeed, no mistakes so coarse as those of the clever cynic in dealing with a man of plain average intellect and more than average honesty, and the fury of a woman scorned is mild resentment compared with the rage of the practised deceiver who is outwitted by mere integrity. Each little world has its own code of honour, often monstrously at variance with the code of the great world. To the able diplo-matists of Berlin Viscount Grey was not playing "cricket" when he used words to express his thoughts. They could have forgiven him had he lied and lost. They might have felt less bitterly had he lied and won. But they hate him above all others because, so to speak, he hit diplomatically below the belt, and used truth as a knuckleduster. To them he is the supreme liar by virtue of an unprofessional veracity.

We cannot regret that a man who represents the highest type of English character was in charge of our affairs during the years of disturbed equilibrium that preceded the war. We may have much to lament; we have nothing to blush for. It is a proud thing for our nation that, while every addition to our know-ledge of those years throws into blacker relief the dishonesty of the Jew and Junker combinations of Berlin and Vienna, the spotless integrity of Viscount Grey, like a snowclad mountain when dawn is chasing night away, reveals itself more dazzling with each increase of light. But it might have been better for England and Europe if that English straightforward-ness had been modified by another quality. Viscount Grey's mind is wholly innocent of irony. He went to the European fair with something of the guilelessness of Moses Primrose when he invested in the gold-rimmed spectacles. The German cynics were foolish to deny the existence of gold; but there is something to be said for a healthy scepticism. Viscount Grey was a little too much impressed by the undeniable shagreen spectacle cases. He was a shade too gentlemanly to apply an acid test to the spectacle rims.

The truth is that, with the highest qualities of his caste, he has some of its defects. Though capable of much work, he is constitutionally indolent. It is astonishing, indeed, in view of his character and circumstances, that he was ever induced to shoulder the great burden he bore for ten years. Of vulgar ambition he possesses no trace, and the objects of a healthy ambition were his without effort. With ample possessions, a pedigree more noteworthy than that of any but a dozen noble families, a singularly sane and wholesome temperament, tastes that demanded no more than his patrimony could easily supply, there was every reason that a life of dignified obscurity should handsomely suffice him. Patriotism, friendship, or what not turned the scale of his inclinations, but his character remained. He did his work, but not as a workman who loves his work as a mistress. With unequalled experience, he was always something of the amateur. He did not even trouble to acquire the tourist's knowledge of foreign countries. He never went abroad; he fished instead. He understood only French, and did not speak that. What was more important, he lacked that instinctive understanding of the European mind which in some Foreign Ministers has compensated for the want of first-hand knowledge.

Looking through his despatches, he saw Grey where another would have detected red, or black, or Imperial purple. To him there was one Grey at the Quai d'Orsay, another in the Wilhelmstrasse, another in the Balplatz—all English Greys, as upright, as limited, as wholly reasonable. That peculiarly English quality which may be described as cosy aloofness was his; the quality which made us look on our island as an anchored ship and the few miles of Channel as an impassable barrier against the envy of less happy lands. His judgment of European problems was coloured by the assumption that the superiority of our moral and physical position rendered us immune. We see him often busy on the circumference of the problem—Agadir and the like—up to the last dreadful disillusionment. There is no evidence that he reached the heart of the matter, that he recognized that Britain might, instead of acting the part of dignified referee, have to fight for very life.

It was, after all, the common heritage from the Victorian time, this notion that alone among nations Great Britain was safe : safe to attack, if the mood took her, safe from being attacked. If Viscount Grey failed to estimate in time the full perils of his policy, it is his glory that he did not shrink from them when they were revealed. To his sense of honourable obligation, and perhaps also to his youth—for he was not old enough to be under the full spell of the Victorian tradition—the nation owes it that it trod from the first the rude and thorny path of duty. Had he blenched, he would no doubt have turned the scales in favour of an unrighteous and precarious neutrality, and we should be to-day paying the full price of that betrayal.

After all allowance is made, some criticism seems justified of the rather nerveless policy pursued by the Asquith Cabinet before the war, a policy for which we know, on the authority of Prince Lichnowsky, Viscount Grey was responsible. Of the petulant outcry raised against him for his course during the earlier war period it is difficult to speak with moderation. The house that is building is not as the house that is built. In the security of the American alliance it is easy to forget that in dealing with a people so legally (and indeed legalistically) minded as the Americans, an arbitrary policy might have repeated, with fatal results, the tragedy of 1812. The impartial historian will probably decide that Viscount Grey, by courteous inflexibility on essentials and by concession in all doubtful cases, gained as much as we could reasonably expect during that critical period before Germany had wholly alienated American opinion.

A few months ago all this discussion might well appear unprofitable. Viscount Grey's career seemed to be closed. Judgment on it seemed to be an affair for more leisurely times. But there are signs of some reaction against the hurried verdict of 1916, and it is well that the man who may yet be called on to undertake great tasks—he must be called before he comes—should be seen in a dry light. He is not what we ordinarily understand as a great man. He lacks the showier qualities. He has no power of compelling speech. He wields not the bejewelled scimitar of Mr. Lloyd George, nor the active rapier of Mr. Balfour, nor the trenchant Roman blade of Mr. Asquith. In sheer intellectual power he must yield to many of his contemporaries. Even in the day of his greatest prestige it was difficult to point to any specific superiority, character apart, in explanation of his unique position in England and Europe.

But Viscount Grey is an example of the truth that a man may be larger than the sum of his qualities. If, he is not a great man, he is certainly a great Englishman. His chief weakness as a Foreign Minister was that he was too English. It is, I think, his chief strength to-day. He stands for English justice, English moderation, English avoidance of extremes. The world knows exactly what he means when he speaks of a League of Nations—that he is neither chasing a sentimental will-o'-the-wisp nor fashioning an instrument of permanent oppression for the defeated. The English people know what he means when he avows himself a democrat while leading the life of an aristocratic recluse. For they see in him more than in most of his contemporaries that old liberality which so long made the English oligarchy almost popular. It may be that the world is doomed to a worse anarchy than that which germinated the seeds of the present desolation. It may be that this country is destined to suffer the pangs of intestinal strife as well as the cleaner wounds of foreign war., But if those calamities are to be avoided it is to men at once sanely democratic and wholesomely conservative that we must look for leadership, and of that type this country possesses no greater example than the clean-souled and high-minded statesman who pained many of his friends for the first and last time when he consented to become the first Viscount Grey of Fallodon.

LORD ROBERT CECIL

CONCERNING Lord Robert, the most important fact is that he is a Cecil. Next in importance is the circumstance that he happens to be a lawyer. He is, for better or worse, the thrall of the family temperament. But he is also a Cecil trained to an exacting and in some senses a liberalizing craft.

Every Cecil is a Cecil before everything. In no English family does the type remain more constant. There have been Cecils good and bad, brilliant and stupid, fools and men of great qualities, if never quite of the greatest. But running through ten generations are discernible certain mental traits a good deal more enduring than any physical feature.

I have read somewhere that the founder of this distinguished house was a prosperous linen-draper who "cut" his trade and turned squire. If so, we may be pretty sure that he was an industrious apprentice of a type very different from the Hogarthian prig.

His eyes might be fixed firmly on the main chance and the master's daughter; he might go to church with exemplary regularity; but that would not prevent his playing tricks incompatible with copybook perfection.

Five qualities are hereditary in the Cecils : a certain lordly care for the interests of the Cecils themselves which would be indelicate in men of lesser breed; a passionate attachment to the Church; an instinct of compromise which enables them, while maintaining the extreme Tory position, to avoid the reproach of mere bigotry; a detachment which would savour of pure arrogance were it not allied with considerable simplicity of manners; and a singular vein of grave rowdiness which breaks out in every generation.

Macaulay has remarked upon the great Burleigh's tendency to practical jokes when he lay at Gray's Inn, and observes that to the last he was "somewhat jocose." Only a very flexible statesman could have saved his head and his fortune under Edward VI., Lady Jane Grey, and Mary, to rise at once to greatness with the accession of Elizabeth. Only a very zealous Protestant could have kept his reputation for passionate orthodoxy after going regularly to Mass while the fires of Smithfield were burning. And Burleigh's integrity, no less than his care for future Cecils, was shown by the circumstance that he left behind him " only " three hundred distinct landed properties, though by improper practices he could have amassed a much larger fortune.

The great Lord Salisbury was Burleigh on a somewhat contracted stage. He had his period of squib-writing at the Temple and of "ragging" in the House. He helped the Church and his family where he could. He stood quite aloof, and still retained a certain popularity. He killed more "Liberal measures" than any man, and yet contrived never to bring about a life-and-death fight between Lords and Commons.

Mr. Balfour, though only half a Cecil, inherited much of the Cecil character. His Fourth Party insubordination, his gay tyranny in Ireland, his constant patronage of a Church with which he has little intellectual sympathy, the taste for dialectical horseplay which he shows even at an advanced age, his capacity for escaping from every cul-de-sac prepared for him by Free Traders and Tariff Reformers, the kindness to kin which led him to shower places and pensions among deserving Cecils, all derive from the original Burleigh; "fair" (when it was quite convenient) and "free" (with the pickings of office).

Of the great Victorian Cecil's sons, none has yet achieved a place in which full play can be given to all the Cecilian characteristics. Lord Hugh is still in the tadpole stage, and Lord Robert is only just emerging. The present Marquis looks as if he would never emerge. But that they are true Cecils in every respect their record has already made clear.

Mr. Gardiner's story of Lord Hugh gravely complaining to his mother of the Socinian tendencies of his nurse is excellent, but obviously inadequate. Had his five-year-old lordship really suspected heresy in that quarter, he would assuredly have adopted a quite different formula of exorcism. He would have put mustard in nurse's tea, kicked her shins, laid booby traps for her, screamed and plunged, and made her life impossible. For, while there is no question of the sincerity of the Cecilian affection for "religion orthodox" members of the family have no objection to "apostolic blows and knocks" for its sake. They will use in the defence of the Establishment all the dodges of a welshing bookmaker to secure his evil gains. Let an impious politician lay hands on the holy ark, and the Cecils are not willing to leave him to Divine vengeance. Trip him up, butt him in the waistcoat, pull his hair, call his grandmother names; nothing is amiss in dealing with the heretic.

These are qualities not altogether amiable. If they
were the only Cecilian qualities, or even if the Hugh-
ligan cast were predominant in the family character,
there would be little to distinguish its cadets from
dozens of mere partisan rowdies. But if they sometimes do not care to remember that they are hereditary
gentlemen, the Cecils seldom permanently forget that
they are hereditary statesmen. And this is conspicuously the case with Lord Robert.

It is with something like a shock that one recalls
that he is fifty-three. That is another peculiarity with
the Cecils—their premature antiquity and their pro-
longed immaturity. Lord Robert was never young,
and he grows old with difficulty. His political salad
days had scarcely ended when he accepted the sober-
ing burden of office. It seems but yesterday that he
was engaged on the Marconi hunt, which he enjoyed
perhaps as a chase even more than as a political purity
crusade, though, to do him justice, he was probably as
shocked as most people with the " indelicacies " he
was probing. Marconi was not in the Cecilian grand
manner; when a Cecil jobs he does it with a stately
disregard of common opinion which robs the thing of
any suggestion of turpitude.

Those who saw it will always remember Lord
Robert's face when Mr. Asquith's name cropped up
in that inquiry. Mention was made of a certain letter
written by the Prime Minister. The gaunt pale
features of Lord Robert flushed with excitement; he
humped his shoulders almost to deformity; the little
tuft produced by the friction of his wig fairly stood
upright; his long neck emerged from his rather loose
collar until he gave the impression of some bird of the
vulture species scenting a new feast. I believe there
is such a thing as a Secretary bird. Lord Robert
looked like that, or at lowest like an Under-Secretary
bird.

His disappointment was painful when the letter was

read! It turned out to run something like this:
"How dull everything is; nothing in the papers but
Winston."

The artless innocence of that letter was a real blow
to Lord Robert. Not that he hated Mr. Asquith, but
it would be such fun to harpoon a victim of that
dignity. It was precisely the same spirit that barbed
his father's attacks on Gladstone: "The right honourable gentleman reminds me of a pettifogging attorney.
(Oh, oh!) I beg the House's pardon. I have done
a great injustice to an honourable profession."

But there was just as much of the paternal Salisbury
in the resolution with which Lord Robert and his
brother went out into the wilderness over Tariff
Reform. Others might bow the knee to the Birmingham Rimmon; they must be excused. Excommunica-
tions descended harmless on them. They lost their
seats and their tempers, but they stuck to their principles. That, again, is the Cecil way. If there is the
possibility of making the best of both worlds, the
Cecils have no ambition for martyrdom. Burleigh
thought his head worth a mass, and his son bemoaned
that " 'Tis a great task to prove one's honesty without
marring one's fortune." But on some subjects honesty
must be proved, though there be as many Chamber-
lains as there are iron plates in Birmingham.

This disinterestedness was the more obvious because
for the brothers there could be no question of a change
of allegiance, as in the case of Mr. Churchill. They
were more bitter Tories without a party than with one.
The Cecil shawl could never be degraded by an alien
fringe, Celtic or otherwise. So they scratched and
kicked and screamed at friend and foe until Ireland,
the Church in Wales, and other questions came to
heal the breach.

At the beginning of the war the two lost sheep had
fairly got back to the home pasture, though hardly to
the fold. But even so late as the formation of the

Coalition there were not a few Unionists who resented Lord Robert's inclusion, just as there were many Marconi-mindful Radicals equally hostile. It is a proof of the statesmanlike capacity which underlies the more debatable elements of the Cecil character that Lord Robert has lived down the latter prejudice much more completely than the former. His only bitter critics are the former Die-hards, who are now Fight-hards, in the sense that they want the fight to be as hard as possible. They decry him because we are not now at war with America over a spirited blockade stroke, because he has grasped the truth that England and English interests are not the sole elements in this world struggle, because he has declared wholeheartedly for Mr. Wilson's policy.

All this, say his detractors, argues the spirit of the trimmer, and Lord Robert is reminded of what his great ancestor would have done. Of course, the great ancestor would have done precisely the same. He did, in fact, much the same. His whole virtue as a statesman was a caution that never relaxed, a prudence that was never tempted. That moderation which used the rack as seldom as possible, and only " as gently as such an uncivil thing could be used," also preserved England from the fearful dangers to which a reckless genius might have exposed her.

Lord Robert has shown a similar understanding of the position and powers of this country. His lawyer training has only strengthened a transmitted instinct for temperance in claim and tenacity in negotiation. His various replies to German pretensions have been admirable in tone and matter. He has faults of style, but he keeps them for the smaller occasions. He has all the limitations of his caste and temperament, but he does not allow them to interfere with a broad judgment on the great questions. He would prefer an England on the old pattern in a world such as we knew before the war. But his Toryism is at least con-

servative; it aims at preserving. And Lord Robert
sees clearly that unless the world is to go a very long
way back it must take a considerable step forward;
there is no staying still.

This perception is the explanation of a success
which has grown steadily more apparent. Lord
Robert has shown himself an excellent man of business in his Department; he is also the one recruit to
the Government who has given promise of much
higher things. For him the party truce has been a
reality; against the arch-conspirator of old days
attaches no suspicion of entering into personal or
party intrigue. He was loyal to Mr. Asquith, because
Mr. Asquith, for the time, represented for him
England alone. He is loyal to his present chief for
no better or worse reason. Until the present business
is over, he is neither Whig nor Tory, but a British
Minister. And he sees much farther than most of his
colleagues. His main defect probably is that his
vision is too telescopic. He understands, like Mr.
Balfour, the necessity of solidarity with world-
democracy. It is yet doubtful whether he has come
to understand that there must be a fuller expression
of democracy at home.

After all, he is the son of the statesman who described an Indian Member of Parliament as a " black
man," and thought the English people would be more
interested in a circus than any extension of local self-
government. He is the brother of Lord Hugh, who
once said that no labouring man wanted a bathroom.
He lives, in short, physically in St. John's Wood, but,
morally, within the palings of the ancestral park.

Lord Robert has all the Cecil indifference to dress,
all the Cecil absence of personal affectation. With
his soft hat, black coat, and light trousers he might
pass for a Socialist intellectual. But there is a hard
core of aristocratic exclusiveness beneath. He typi-
fies that old house at Hatfield, which, on the very

verge of Greater London, is far more distant from the Londoner than Chatsworth or Eaton Hall.

He will probably miss true greatness through this detachment, which is one of the Cecil heirlooms. But he is destined, doubtless, to go much further. Of all the new men in the Government his is the solitary figure which suggests large possibilities.

MR. BALFOUR

AMONG the writer's most vivid memories is that of a dull meeting in a dull room in a dull street in the City of London, looking its dullest in the gloom of a late autumn afternoon nearly seven years ago.

Mr. Balfour, after defying for years the slings and arrows of outrageous Tariff enthusiasts, had decided on abdication. In a speech of great dignity he gave an account of the stewardship he was about to surrender. He had reached an age, he said, when it was commonly supposed that the powers of the mind and will were on the wane. He could not honestly say he had noticed any signs of degeneration in his own case, but he was no impartial judge, and must bow to the general sentiment that the leadership of the party should be placed in younger and more vigorous hands.

The full irony of this valedictory oration was not appreciated until, after an agitated interval, Mr. Bonar Law reigned in Mr. Balfour's stead. Perhaps it is not wholly appreciated still. For the conquerors in the fight which Mr. Balfour had lost were wholly innocent of irony. Had the dragon beaten St. George it would no doubt have munched him without the smallest suspicion that the dinner might be something greater than the diner. With the same stolid gusto the Confederates triumphed over their fallen leader. It was the victory of the simple over the complex, of an eager empiricism over a doubting philosophy. Mr. Balfour fell because, like that very complete English Tory, Hamlet, he was only sure of the disadvantages of every course of action, and on the whole would rather endure the ills he had than fly to others that he knew not of. With almost all the gifts that make men great, he had one fatal disqualification for the leadership of the Conservative Party as it existed in 1911. He was a true conservative. And the Conservative Party was then everything but conservative. The last thing it wanted was to stand still. It was possessed by a Gadarene frenzy for advance, and Mr. Balfour's offence was that he would not lead decisively down the steep places of its desire.

To a superficial view at this time, Mr. Balfour's career, however brilliant, must have given the predominating impression of failure. The memory of the Irish Secretaryship had faded; events, too, were daily giving a decisive though belated answer to that talented essay in repression; the Irish problem might not be insoluble, but certainly twenty years of resolute government had not solved it. As to Mr. Balfour's later career, the party under his leadership had gone to pieces; his authority had vanished; he, the champion of Parliamentary fence, had been worsted by the plain claymore of "C.-B."; his personal prestige had been dimmed by the blaze of Mr. Chamberlain's glory. Men had begun to speak of him as a philosopher. There is only one lower level for an English statesman of undeniable intellectual standing. It is to be called a doctrinaire.

The war, however, has led to a general revaluation, and Mr. Balfour's is one of the few reputations that has constantly risen. True, this appreciation is confined to a somewhat narrow circle, and applies only to the more obvious aspects of Mr. Balfour's work, his American mission, and so forth. For full justice he will have to await the deliverance of posterity. But

5

the guess may be ventured that when all these vast
transactions have fallen into historic perspective his
will be one of the two or three great figures emerging
from the crowd of small and very small men. At
present we are too near the canvas to see the picture;
at the proper distance touches that seem irrelevant
and even grotesque will probably fall together as in
a masterpiece of Velasquez.

For example, that brilliant duel with Mr. Chamberlain, with all its incomparable skill, seems to the eye
of a contemporary pure futility. Mr. Balfour aimed
at preserving party unity, and split his party hope-
lessly. He tried to establish a common formula, and
actually succeeded in evolving half a dozen mutually
hostile cliques. He steered his barque with marvellous
skill past numberless snags, only to run it on a sand-
bank in the end. All this is incomprehensible --
remembering that we are dealing with a man of first-
rate mind and great Parliamentary talent—if we
consider Mr. Balfour only as a British statesman with
a vital interest in the fiscal question. It is easily
explicable if we view him as a Gallio on the issue
between Cobdenism and Chamberlainism, but also as
the one British statesman of European mind, chiefly
intent on the enormous European problem then shap-
ing. Just about the time Mr. Chamberlain launched
his Tariff campaign, Mr. Balfour discerned the new
tendencies on the Continent, and took the first steps to
meet them. His delaying tactics on the Tariff controversy, his calm endurance of party insubordination,
his insensibility to ridicule and blindness to electoral
warnings, may be understood if we also grasp that
time was essential to confirm the new orientation in our
foreign policy, and that it was precisely for time for
this object that he was fighting.

His "weakness" at a later period is explicable on
similar assumptions. He wished to protect the
"rights" of property. He desired to guard the in-

terests of the Church. He was determined if possible
to prevent Home Rule. But he knew where to stop.
He might use Carsonism; he would not be its instrument. Mr. Balfour can only be understood if we
recognize in him a dual personality. He has the
mind and spirit of a great European statesman in the
body of a rather limited English Tory. His broader
self belongs rather to the Richelieus than the Pitts;
Parliamentary successes notwithstanding, his subtle
brain better fits the closet than the Senate. His
smaller personality finds its spiritual home with the
genteel inhabitants of Cheltenham. On more philosophical grounds he shares the prejudices of the half-
pay major and the cultivated rentier.

Mr. Balfour's lack of sympathy with democratic
ideals is, in fact, based on something less robust than
the Cecilian arrogance. It is rather the shrinking of
a provincial blue-stocking from what she considers
"vulgar." Mr. Balfour's low vitality may have as
much to do with it as his mental fastidiousness. But
his conscious objection to democracy would seem
to be based on a fear that the pleasanter things of
life—art, literature, cultivated manners, personal
distinction—would be obliterated if privilege disappeared. For the mass of men he seems to feel there
is no possibility of advance; the democratic flood
would not fructify the deserts, but only obliterate the
oases. There is not enough culture to go round; why
lose what we have in a vain attempt to give everyone
his share?

This frame of mind is no more responsive to the cry
for liberty than to that for democratic equality. The
subordination of inferior to superior races—right of
definition being one of the privileges of superiority—
is logically connected with the subordination of class
to class. Mr. Balfour's attitude to the "Celtic fringe"
springs from this same notion of the world as a wilderness with a few cosy corners. Hundreds of kindly

pagans in Roman days held much the same views, and justified slavery and the subjugation of nations on similar grounds. To say that Mr. Balfour was content with the old Europe, any more than with the old England, would no doubt be profoundly untrue; he is far too intelligent and honest to be satisfied with the pretences that lull the consciences of ordinary people of the comfortable class. But though it was no doubt all profoundly unsatisfactory, would stirring up the hell-broth improve matters? As with all his class, *quieta non movere* was to him the highest wisdom. The *status quo* was the true aim of statesmanship, and to him, as to Hamlet, the "cursed spite" of his fate was that the times were so out of joint as to compel some readjustment.

Being the man he is, it is to the credit of Mr. Balfour that, under the shock of reality, he has had the candour to revise his judgment. He does not like democracy, but he accepts it, bad as it may be, as better than Cæsarism as it is now revealed. He accepted the formula of Dr. Wilson, and he has adhered to it, despite the set-back that doctrine suffered in some quarters through the follies of Bolshevism. The mental habits of a lifetime are hard to break, and there are occasions when Mr. Balfour suggests that if we are to have the spirit of democracy it must not be taken "neat." He is an autocrat in his own department, and a very Metternich in his enthusiasm for the sacredness of diplomatic mysteries. But no man is straighter or sterner on the main issue, and none can be found to unite such dexterity of method with such rigidity of principle.

It was quite without feeling against Germany that Mr. Balfour set about his great work in laying the foundations of the Entente. Like most educated Englishmen, he was rather inclined to German culture, and not a little tolerant to Prussian ambitions. The Treaty referred to in Prince Lichnowsky's memoir shows how far he was ready to go in order to preserve the relations of the Victorian time. When compelled to new courses, he had no more animus against Germany than a mathematician, in calculating the trajectory of a new gun, has against friction and the force of gravitation. He was merely taking precautions as chief trustee of the British Commonwealth.

But his blood, if anything too cold and temperate, has been stirred deeply by the events of the war. He has the more loathing for the Prussian doctrine of force, because he was at one time rather apt to admire in its less hideous manifestations. As a well-bred man he is repelled by German arrogance; as a civilized man, by German barbarity; as a diplomatic man, by German unreason. That quiet stubbornness which has made him, on the whole, a national liability in domestic affairs is, in his present position, a national asset of prime importance. It ensures that perhaps the finest intellectual person in our armoury, guided by a perception of European problems quite unique among Englishmen, will be used without remorse when the time comes for settling the great account.

SIR F. E. SMITH

He should, of course, be called Sir Frederick, but there are two excuses for retaining the familiar initials. In the first place they constitute a subtle kind of compliment, and the sincere critic must in this case be thrifty of all material for compliments. It is something of an achievement for a modern Smith to succeed in impressing his simple initials on the public, and that " F. E." has done so argues a certain stature. All credit to him that he did not try to ease the battle for notoriety by making himself a Roper, Parkinson, Plantagenet, or Montmorency Smith. Perhaps a negative virtue in this matter attaches to godfathers and godmothers, but we all know that their omissions are frequently repaired by the ambitious bearer of a commonplace name.

In the second place, "F. E." seems oddly suited to our Attorney-General; much better suited than his inexplicable baronetcy. It might, like its owner, stand for anything. It combines challenge and reserve, the adroit union of which is largely the secret of "F. E.'s" success. It suggests the artful modesty of a clever coquette, who knows that she can sell best when she gives nothing away. Men can often be judged better (the graphologists notwithstanding) by what they sign rather than by how they sign themselves, and the letters "F. E." are quite symbolical.

"Dost know this water-fly?" Hamlet's words come trippingly to the tongue when one contemplates a career like this. Osric, the point-device courtier, is the eternal type of the ephemeral. With as much difficulty one associates the idea of immortality with "F. E." It irks Osric not at all to change his views. He describes the weather one moment as "indifferent cold," and the next as "very sultry," for no better reason than Hamlet will have it so. And in this he only anticipates "F. E.'s" attitude to the British electorate.

Osric had "only got the tune of the time and outward habit of encounter." Nobody ever suspected "F. E." of more. Osric knew nothing of the deeper causes of the quarrel, but was enormously interested in the mere rapier play and the swords themselves, finding them "very dear to the fancy, very responsive to the hilts, most delicate carriages, and of a very liberal conceit." "F. E." is equally bored by the deeper things in the minds of combatants, and equally immersed in the millinery and upholstery of the lists. He is a judge of "palpable hits," no judge at all of things real enough to be impalpable.

Finally Osric was "spacious in the possession of dirt"; "F. E." must be doing well, too. For we must not think of the water-fly merely as a type of significance. It is also the most agile, energetic, and voracious of creatures, with a great instinct for the nourishment of its slim and elegant form. While it seems to be just dancing for joy of the thing it keeps its hundred-lensed eye on the main chance. Really, the further the similitude develops the better it pleases. For example, how quickly the water-fly passes through the stages from grubdom to maturity! And it stings.

"F. E." stings. His sting is perhaps his chief feature; at any rate he owes to it most of the greatness that has descended upon him and now threatens, extinguisher-like, to press him down altogether. By virtue of it he has become Attorney-General, a baronet of the United Kingdom, a Bencher of his Inn, one of His Majesty's Counsel officially (and therefore, of course, accurately) described as learned in the law, a Privy Councillor, and a Lieutenant-Colonel in the Army. By vice of it he may yet have a fall. But thus far the capacity of uttering pungent impromptus, the rarer capacity of sitting up half the night to invent them, has brought to the briefless barrister of twelve years or so ago all the outward show of greatness. Examining this pomp a little closely we may detect signs of Master Shallow's borrowed doublet stuffed out with straw; but the world is not over-critical, and there are, perhaps, some who still think "F. E." a great statesman and a profound lawyer. But the first class are now sparely represented at Westminster, and the second have never inhabited the Temple.

The bubble of "F. E.'s" reputation was blown by a single emission of the breath, though heaven alone knows what anxious thought went to the compounding of the parent mixture. There are secrets of political alchemy that must be jealously kept from the vulgar. Like Disraeli, whom he took for his model, "F. E." became famous through a single speech. It was not a very good speech. Read in cold blood to-day it is found not a little schoolboyish in its studied provocation, its sixth-form satire, and its elegantly insincere scorn. Only those who heard it can understand why, when the slim, well-tailored, dandyish young man with the long, pale face and the arrogant lips had sat down in a tumult of cheers, the lobbies buzzed with excited wonderment over the discovery of a new fighting leader on the Unionist side.

But if the speech was in no sense that of a great man, however immature, it was eminently that of a very clever tactician. It acted like a charm on the small Unionist remnant that had escaped the rout of 1906. In its gay insolence and cheery defiance it contrasted brilliantly with the savage gloom of Mr. Chamberlain and the depressing fatalism of Mr. Balfour. It restored the instinct of fight—especially important in the case of men with nothing very obvious to fight for. Nobody believes now—perhaps few believed even then—that the young M.P. for Walton spoke from anywhere far behind his teeth. But the sick man inclines rather to the quack who gives him an energizer than to the physician who recommends a long course of low living, and " F. E.," though largely responsible for leading the Tory Party through strange places, was remembered only for the draught that revived while it poisoned.

The young lawyer had treated the House of Commons like a jury, with a single eye to the verdict, and he got it. Two worlds were henceforth his oyster. The briefs came trooping gaily to his chambers, and there was little he might not hope for in politics if only the Liberal majority could be whittled away to nothing. The levity with which he went about the task of reduction can only be explained by reference to the habits of water-flies. They may incidentally enjoy stinging, buzzing, and darting from point to point; but all these things have a quite definite purpose; if water-flies possess no very consistent theory of life they have a deep-seated instinct for living.

It is only just to admit that "F. E." played a big and dangerous game with great skill. But he is, for all that, hardly a player in the great manner. Spiritually, he has affinities with the Churchills, father and son; he is all for the legitimate gamble. But he does not stake his shirt on a number at the roulette table, though he might perhaps stake an indifferent party's whole wardrobe; he is rather for "first and third dozen" and other games where, if you have a cool head and a system, you may win a good deal, and can hardly be ruined. The Scottish lord in "The Fortunes of Nigel" had the same talent, and acquired something of the same reputation. For by this time nobody quite trusts "F. E." He is too cautiously violent to please his friends or to terrify his foes.

"F. E." is a daredevil with reservations. For pretty well any cause he is ready to die in the last ditch, but he holds himself free to decide which is the last ditch, and how the final sacrifice shall be made. It would really be very interesting to know exactly what Sir Edward Carson, who has none of this light Jesuitry, thinks of him to-day. Five years ago "F. E." was gallantly conjugating the verb "to gallop." "You gallop; they gallop; let us all gallop; but especially I will gallop." There never was so mad a fellow since Master Shallow lay at Clement's Inn. Others might occasionally shiver at the idea of civil strife in earnest. It is only right to suppose that the Londonderrys and Carsons sometimes had misgivings. Not so our doughty Templar. He was always buoyant. "Civil war—certainly. Red ruin and the breaking up of laws—why, my dear sir, wait till we get really well started. Of course it will be a nuisance—I shall probably have to give up my huntin'—but if the Rads persist, something must flow. I hope it will not be human gore."

Yet " F. E.," with all his anxiety to burn his boats, worked hard to insure them before applying the torch. Probably no man had moments of more acute anxiety in 1914, when it seemed possible that he must either gallop in earnest or betray; no man, it is safe to say, more sincerely welcomed the Party truce which gave him an opportunity of getting safely out of his Ulster saddle. Since then there is no evidence that he has given a second thought to his dear and dour friends.

I was once defending our political system against a cynic. I held, perhaps rashly, that principles still counted. My friend at once asked : " What particular principle does ' F. E.'—who is a very typical politician —stand for ?" And I was at a loss to answer. There may be points, hitherto unrevealed, on which he feels deeply. Perhaps he is not entirely happy with his party ; he has sometimes given hints of a languid speculative preference for a less negative creed. Some truth there may be in the old story that he tossed with Sir John Simon at Oxford as to which side each should take, as one party could not contain both. "F. E." lost, and went in for Unionism. Certainly his success has been bought at a not inconsiderable price. Conservatism always treats its leaders as valets, and more than once " F. E." has been made to feel his position in conflict with the Wellbore-Wellbores of his party. He is a proud man and a sensitive, and such earn all they get in this employment.

Still, it may be well doubted if he is fit for any other. There is one infallible touchstone to-day for men of affairs. Are they mere creatures of the moment, or have they some touch with the eternal ? Their attitude towards the full policy of President Wilson—its refusal to parley with evil no less than its search for a healing formula—distinguishes statesmen as the sheep are separated from the goats. Every fool can point out the difficulties of that policy, but every truly wise man knows that those difficulties must either be conquered, or they will conquer mankind.

Sir F. E. Smith left his not unimportant office as chief legal adviser to the Crown to go propagandizing in America. He returned in circumstances of some mystery. According to his own published statements his mission was wholly a success. Yet there are those who still doubt. They base their judgment on no isolated incident, but on the general incompatibility of so light a temperament with the tremendous earnestness of the great Republic.

MR. BONAR LAW

THERE is no very obvious connection between Mr. Bonar Law and the Ancient Mariner. Yet the last time I saw the Leader of the House of Commons, a depressed figure on the Treasury Bench, somehow suggesting in his gloomy preoccupation a political Eugene Aram with moral gyves upon his wrists, the lines of Coleridge came unbidden to my mind :

> " Like one that on a lonesome road
> Doth walk in fear and dread,
> And, having once turned round, walks on,
> And turns no more his head ;
> Because he knows a frightful fiend
> Does close behind him tread."

It is of that fiend which dogs Mr. Law in his earnest attempts to walk straight that one must mostly speak in dealing with him. As the case of Ireland reminds us, the chief importance of the past is that it is nine-tenths of the present. It would be a pleasant task to discuss Mr. Bonar Law only as a war Minister. We could then speak of him as one who has worked, not always wisely, but well; we could acknowledge cheerfully that of the few politicians who have emerged from the great test with enhanced reputations he is one; we could pay tribute to his loyalty to engagements, his unselfish co-operation with men he has never liked, his acquiescence in measures little to his taste, his honest desire to sink all personal prejudices for the common cause.

Certainly such commendation would be given with due qualification. Mr. Law is in no sense a great Minister. His abilities, though useful, are eminently ordinary. The whole tone of his mind is commonplace. He lacks almost every essential of a leader of men, and has often shown himself unequal to the quite measurable task of controlling that small mob of men called the House of Commons. But, on the other hand, he is, according to his lights, thoroughly straightforward, and not, as politicians go, a self-seeker. If there were only his war record to be considered, little need be said of him. Decent mediocrity is a sterile text.

But, unhappily, the main fact concerning Mr. Bonar Law is not himself. It is not the haunted man, but the thing that haunts him, that matters most. It is the fiend, not the constrained wayfarer, that occupies the centre of our picture. To drop parable, it would be a very small matter whether Mr. Bonar Law, as a human individual, remained to pursue his course of small usefulness in the Government, or made way for someone not much better or much worse. But during all these months of war there has been a fearful danger involved in his relations to his party and his party's relations to Sir Edward Carson.

That danger has been aggravated by the very honesty which is one of the most agreeable features of Mr. Law's character. " The construction of his mind," says a witty observer, " has no shadows, or ingle-nooks, or cosy corners." He is upright and downstraight, without a savour of *double entendre* in

his nature, innocent of artifice in little things as well
as great. It was his large innocence, more than anything else, that delivered Mr. Law into the hands of
the Carsonites, and has kept him there. Mr. Balfour
had for years played with Ulster, as he had played
with Tariff Reform, without committing himself. Mr.
Law had scarcely assumed the leadership before Mr.
Asquith could truly say that the new "dogma of
anarchy" had been "countersigned by all the leading
men of the Tory Party."

Very skilfully Sir Edward Carson transferred from
his own shoulders to those of an English statesman the
burden of responsibility for everything that might
happen, until at last Mr. Law was definitely pledged
to support Ulster in her resistance to Home Rule,
even though the keeping of that pledge might involve
"something more than making speeches." Such was
the situation before the war. It would be ungracious
and mischievous to recall these facts if the past were
not still very much the present. The pledge, given
with reckless straightforwardness, was not withdrawn
when the Ulster lunacy was dwarfed by a greater peril.
Instead of making himself a free man, Mr. Law, misled by that imperious integrity of his, bound himself
with new fetters. Having tied his party hand and
foot to the chariot of Sir Edward Carson, he proceeded
to bind himself with chains as tyrannous to his party.
He entered the Coalition pledged to retain office only
so long as the majority of the party approved of his
leadership. The consequences have been seen, or
rather felt, during more than three unhappy years.
Nobody took the party truce more seriously than Mr.
Bonar Law. None tried more consistently to observe
it in letter and spirit. None risked more, in personal
position, for it. But he failed to take the only steps
which could have made his good intentions really
operative. He did not free himself or his party from
the past. The party—or rather that section of it which

has usurped power—has followed Sir Edward Carson, and Mr. Law has followed the party.

Enough has already happened to show how great a misfortune was the absence of strength, sanity, and self-control in the Tory leadership during those fateful years before the war. But for the Ulster alliance, indeed, the whole course of events during the past four years might have been different. Blame lies on all parties and on nearly all individuals, but the heaviest indictment at the bar of history must be answered by one man. On Sir Edward Carson rests much responsibility for all the blood spilt in the Sinn Fein rebellion, for the wrecking of all the fair hopes of Irish unity, for the loss of Irish battalions, for grave moral injury to the Allied cause, and—to descend from the great to the very small—for the mutilation of Mr. Bonar Law's public usefulness.

It may be questioned, however, whether, even apart from this malign influence, Mr. Law is fitted for any great share in such a struggle as the present. His modest parts might suffice if they were reinforced by great and animating ideals. But Mr. Law unites a hot head with cold feet. There is a sterilizing touch of pessimism in his character. He may have large charity. He has little faith or hope. He confessed once that he was an "enthusiast" for Tariff Reform, but it is highly characteristic that he espied the road to that Eldorado in "two bad winters." His enthusiasm for any wider cause is not very obvious. Fighting autocracy, he seems to yield it the tribute of a despairing admiration. Everybody remembers his anticipative dirge (in the form of a vote of congratulation) on the Russian Revolution. It rather resembled the speech of a morose bachelor uncle at a christening : " A fine child, you say. Yes. But I've always heard that the finest children are most susceptible to whooping-cough, measles, thrush, and diphtheria in their infancy, and to consumption, paralysis, and spinal complaints as they grow into adolescence."

How far the Girondists of Russia were helped by this singular (and unhappily prophetic) tribute history does not relate. It certainly depressed the spirits of friends of liberty in England. Some time later, again, Mr. Law indulged in melancholy musings on the futility of that freedom on which President Wilson and others set much store. "Democratic institutions with free Parliaments," he said, "are not the best instruments for carrying on a war." There is an old saying (which happens also to be true) that the bad workman always complains of his tools. Mr. Law surely cannot with grace accuse the weakness of some forms of representative government. Exactly what results Mr. Law would achieve with the powers of a Bismarck must remain a matter of speculation. But it is pretty certain what a Bismarck would have done with Mr. Law himself four or five years ago.

We need not discuss whether Great Britain is really " democratic," or how far the German Government has enjoyed greater freedom than our own to dispose of life and liberty. Certainly no German Minister has dared to impose taxation comparable to that which the House of Commons and the nation have accepted with resignation and even with applause. It is certain, too, that "democratic institutions" have not prevented the United States making war with great vigour. Perhaps Mr. Law means that under our own peculiar system there is no way of dealing with mischievous people who happen to have behind them great social influence or voting power. That characteristic weakness has certainly had signal illustration of late years. But an impeachment of our institutions on such grounds should surely come from another quarter.

This rather suburban cant about the defects of " democracy "—a system yet to be tried in this country—may be simply borrowed from men with a deeper political philosophy than Mr. Law's. He is himself no aristocrat, and, to do him justice, no snob. He does not decry " democracy " on the genteel grounds of a similar faith in Wimbledon or Maidenhead. But he seems to take Carlyle and his " greatman " notions rather more seriously than younger men, and, like most patriots of his generation, is steeped in second-hand and second-rate German thought. Sedan was more than a victory over the French Army ; it was the crowning triumph of the German spirit. For forty years France plunged into pessimism, and England into something worse, a kind of despairing admiration of the pickelhaube in things both material and spiritual. It became the mark of a patriotic Englishman to wish his country more like Germany. The part of an enlightened citizen was to depreciate England and exalt " German methods." In his character of Tariff Reformer Mr. Law followed a bad fashion with special zeal, and it would almost seem that in fighting Germany he has not ceased to admire her. This spirit, so common in our ruling men, happily so rare in the ruled, lies at the root of that servile labouring to follow a German lead which was the most conspicuous and disastrous folly in the earlier stages of the war. Bernhardi has described such imitation of externals as the surest sign of incapacity, and indeed common sense rejects the notion of fighting anything with " its own weapons." As Mr. Chesterton has put it, who scratches a tiger or bites a shark ?

But this lack of sympathy with older English ideas is only part of the general foreignness of Mr. Law's outlook and personality. He refuses to recognize Irish nationality, and really Mr. Dillon is as English as he. He represents the denationalization of English Toryism, as well as its temporary conquest by the merely urban—one might almost say suburban— elements. He has never been regarded by the people who still are the real strength of the Tory Party as

more than a stop-gap. Squiredom and farmerdom
are even yet bewildered (as well they may be) that
this Canadian-born Glasgow iron merchant, landless,
Presbyterian, and teetotal, should stand for them.
Mr. Law occupies a position rather analogous to that
of Lord Rosebery when official head of the Liberal
Party—he is only recognized with reservations. The
ordinary Tory is told that Mr. Law is leader, and must
have his way, and internally answers, like Talleyrand
to the poet, " Je ne vois pas la nécessité." Mr. Law
is uneasily conscious of the essential falsity of his
position; he knows that the unstable equilibrium
resulting from the temporary defeat of Hatfield by
Birmingham cannot indefinitely endure; and this
consciousness is at the root of half the trouble.

A leader more sure of his right would have shaken
himself free of the pledge to the Carsonites; would
never have consented to enter a Cabinet, like a trade
union delegate, with his resignation (so to speak)
written out beforehand; would have been bound by
no instructions in setting out to navigate an un-
charted sea. It may be added that such a leader
would not have consented to Mr. Law's present position in the House of Commons as the mere mouth-
piece of a body consisting mainly of his own nominal
subordinates who sometimes tell him things and sometimes do not. The duties of that anomalous position
he has carried out manfully, and with a certain skill.
His Parliamentary manner has immensely improved
in the process, though he still occasionally lapses into
the "new style" of his Opposition leadership. His
own special work has been well done on the whole.
He is not a great Chancellor of the Exchequer, but
there is a businesslike neatness in his methods, contrasting well with the grandiose messiness of a more
vivid personality.

This efficiency is, indeed, his strong side. In him
industry and cool common sense in some small things

6

contrast oddly with strong delusion in many great things. He is a composite of Don Quixote and Sancho Panza, in which the knightly side is also the prose side. The qualities which make him a useful Minister would never have made him a party leader. The qualities which made him a party leader have led him into entanglements which seriously diminish his usefulness as a Minister.

MR. REGINALD McKENNA

IF, by choice or chance, you should happen to lose yourself behind Westminster Abbey—and there are worse places for the straying philosopher—you are pretty certain to find yourself in Smith Square.

Supposing that you affect only the picturesque, you will get out of it as soon as may be; if you have a leaning to the study of social phenomena the chances are you will be interested. It is not a large square or a handsome one; there is no bloom of old red-brick or freshness of verdure to delight the eye; the houses, handsome in their way, are too new and too exposed to have the delicious cosiness of Cowley Street just round the corner. The Abbey is quite close at hand, but the characteristic flavour of Smith Square is not the dust of medievalism; it is rather straw and grit from the Horseferry Road, and the aroma of manure barges on the river, against which the scents of a new and rather raw civilization maintain a hopeless struggle. Not two hundred yards away is slumdom unmitigated. But Smith Square, save in that matter of flavour, is morally distant as if a broad province lay between. There are certain streets leading from it where you may occupy a house "replete," as the agents say (and we wish they wouldn't), "with every modern convenience," and have for your literal next-door neighbours four hunger-smitten families living in a frowsy tumbledown den. These thoroughfares are passing through the transition stage, which in the case of Smith Square has been happily completed. There the rich middle class has not quite pushed out the proletarian, and must at least recognize his physical existence. In Smith Square it is different; the process is complete. St. John's Wood has as much in common with Lisson Grove as Smith Square with poor Westminster.

At Number 36 lives Mr. Reginald McKenna, late Chancellor of the Exchequer. If you have a nodding acquaintance with Mr. McKenna you might almost pick out the house. It seems extremely natural that Mr. McKenna, model of the high bourgeoisie, and therefore rather farther removed from the common run of men and women than any Sir Leicester Dedlock, should have chosen Smith Square for his town house. But it is more than natural—it seems inevitable—that, having chosen Smith Square, he should live in Number 36. The house is so like him. It is solid, efficient, advantageously placed, built of the very best pressed bricks, irreproachably British, and a little forbidding in its aggressive freshness. Go inside, and you will find every evidence of taste and education; the Persian carpets and the English classics will be of the best; there will be the due touch of old culture to correct the oiled smoothness of modern convenience; and yet—well, if you happen to be fanciful you will feel the grit just as you did outside.

For grit, in both senses, enters into the very being of Mr. Reginald McKenna. He showed grit when he rowed bow for Cambridge in the famous victory of 1887, an occasion as important as any in his life. He showed grit in the years between 1895 and 1906, when he clung to the House of Commons, though the prospects were none too good for a highly practical and go-ahead young man. He showed grit in every office he held. He was a minor success as Financial Secretary to the Treasury. But he did not hesitate to risk this limited reputation by taking the Board of Education after Mr. Birrell had failed to conquer or conciliate the raging clerical. At the Admiralty he stubbornly held his own against those who wanted many Dreadnoughts and those who wanted none. As Home Secretary he bore with stoicism a load of unpopularity which would have crushed a more sensitive man : Suffragists, Labour men, the Bishop of St. Asaph, and the *Daily Mail,* furious crank and fiery anti-Hun, made no impression on his adamantine nerve. Probably he never lost an hour's sleep over all of them. At any rate, he survived to make, as Chancellor of the Exchequer in the first Coalition Ministry, the first businesslike War Budget, and only resigned office when Mr. Asquith was driven out.

Grit, in the complimentary sense, cannot be denied to a statesman with such a record. But Mr. McKenna is gritty in another way; there is something really disconcerting in his matter-of-fact composition. Every writer, sooner or later, refers to the iron hand in the velvet glove. Mr. McKenna's glove is made of emery paper, and there is a scratchiness even in his geniality. His intellect might be geologically classified as old red sandstone. At Cambridge he wooed the "crossgrained muses of the cube and square" with success, but it would be ridiculous to speak of him, as some have done, as a great mathematician. The highest in that kind is not destitute of a kind of poetry, and there is less poetry in Mr. Reginald McKenna than in Mr. Kipling. His mathematics are those of the actuary; there are scores of men in banks and accountants' offices of at least equal attainments. But politicians who go farther than the rule of three are exceptional, and any little aridity there might be in the by-products of Mr. McKenna's mind was compensated by his real understanding of figures. One might summarize the matter by saying that he has succeeded by being something of a man and a good deal of a ready-reckoner. He has never lacked courage of a sort, he has played the party game with more straightness and loyalty than a good many, he hits straight from the shoulder, and he has that happy lack of humour which saves a man from being hurt either by self-criticism or the satires of opponents. On his business side he is methodical in getting up a case, neat in his exposition, and masculine in his contempt for rhetorical fiddle-faddle—unless he avoids it because he knows he could not manage it well. His defects are the complement of his qualities; he lacks breadth, humanity, and enthusiasm; he is more out of touch with life and ideas, than a Blue Book.

Such men often go far under any constitution. There were McKennas in Stuart England and in Bourbon France, whose eminence is a puzzle to the historian exploring in vain all contemporary record to find a single phrase or action to mark them as extraordinary. There are probably McKennas even in China. The type flourishes on the whole better under autocratic conditions; a clever monarch uses men of the kind for his particular purpose, and decisively excludes them as general counsellors; Colbert is given his head in finance, but must not meddle with high policy. Under our system, absurdly enough, a perfect multiplication table of a man has to pretend that he wants more voters or fewer public-houses. Still, there must be in every Government people who do know the drier elements of public business, and it is easy to understand the value set on Mr. McKenna once he had reached the position of a possible Under-Secretary. But, as in the case of the fly in amber, a good many people have wondered how he got there. The story is worth repeating as an illustration of the chancy methods of our political recruiting.

It has been mentioned that young McKenna was

bow in the victorious Cambridge boat in the year 1887.
The late Sir Charles Dilke was as keen on rowing as
on things intellectual and political, and never allowed
a good oar to escape him. McKenna was much on
the Thames after leaving the Cam, and the riverside
intimacy between him and Sir Charles ripened into
one of those pathetic friendships which often subsist
between disappointed men and young people in whom
they see something to remind them of their earlier
selves. Sir Charles and his protégé had a good many
points in common. The elder man possessed vastly
more talent, but the younger one had enough of his
more sober qualities to make patronage a subtle kind
of self-praise. It was a mutual affair, like the somewhat similar friendship of Wycherley and Pope.
Dilke's interest was flattering to a young man fresh
from the University. McKenna's reverence was
soothing to a man of Dilke's bitter experience. Dilke
found, after years of waiting, that though he might
return to the Commons he could not return to official
politics; there were influences too strong to be overcome. He had, however, a hold on the official politicians, and, if he could not get the promise of a place,
the embargo did not apply to his adopted political
son. There was a tacit understanding that when the
opening came the man in readiness should not be
overlooked. Thus it happened that when "C.-B."
took office in 1905 Mr. Reginald McKenna figured in
his first list of Ministers. Had he been thrice the man
he was without that pull, he would have remained
private member for the North Monmouthshire constituency which he has represented for twenty-three
years. With that pull he started on a ladder which
a man of his character and qualifications was bound
to climb.

His talents, such as they were, were highly appreciated by his official chiefs. There is a story that Mr.
Asquith actually appointed Mr. McKenna as Chan-

cellor of the Exchequer when he himself gave up the Treasury on becoming Prime Minister, but that Mr. Lloyd George, jealous of his rights, threatened trouble unless the choice was revoked in his favour. Had Mr. Asquith stood to his guns—assuming the truth of the story—the whole history of the years between 1908 and 1914 might have been different. It is possible for men like Mr. McKenna to create revolutions without knowing it; Grenville, a man of somewhat similar type, actually did so. But he would certainly never have ventured consciously into deep waters. Possibly a quarrel over the Treasury ten years ago may have had its influence on the events of the last month of 1916; possibly it was personal loyalty to Mr. Asquith and nothing more that determined Mr. McKenna's course, and has kept him, unlike Mr. Montagu, steadfast in it. But in any case, it must have been a strain for a man of his temperament to work with one of the Prime Minister's. Mr. Lloyd George in one respect at least resembles Chatham : he does not care a jot for money, and is even proud of the sacrifices he induces the nation to accept. Mr. McKenna thinks chiefly of the price of glories. He has never been credited with an enthusiasm for the war, and, whatever his views on the general question, he has regarded with steady jealousy the claims of the Army, as against those of commerce and industry. It is the cobbler's faith in leather—not to be altogether disregarded, nor yet to be blindly shared.

It was generally believed, when Mr. McKenna accepted the offer of his banking friend, Sir Edward Holden, that he had made his gesture of farewell to politics. Certainly at that time there were grounds for supposing that he was convinced the new world had no place for him. Since he has taken the trouble to correct the rumour, it may be assumed that he retains, or has recovered, faith in the fortunes of official Liberalism and of his own star. Yet it is not easy to see a great place for Mr. McKenna in the politics of the future. He may repeat himself. He can do little more. For of all the " Old Gang "—or, more accurately, that part of it which the present Prime Minister failed to take with him—Mr. McKenna, despite his superficial modernity, is the oldest and the least elastic. There are few administrations in which he could not be useful in a humdrum way. It is impossible to imagine a successful administration, in the times we are likely to see, of which he could be the chief. For a successful chief must understand the national temper, and from the national temper Smith Square is almost more aloof than Lansdowne House.

LORD NEWTON AND OTHERS

THE old lawyers invented dummies to represent substantial plaintiffs and defendants, and it is chiefly as a John Doe or Richard Roe that Lord Newton is here mentioned. The thing he stands for is more important than himself.

Lord Newton is, indeed, of no special importance. It is rather remarkable that, with parts so good, and with a decided inclination for public life, he has done so little. The explanation probably resides equally in his rather flighty temperament and his possession of ample fortune and hereditary rank. Station is rather like a cork waistcoat. It enables heavy, inexpert people to keep afloat who would otherwise infallibly go to the bottom. But it tires and impedes an active man, and prevents him ever developing into a first-class swimmer. Men like Lord Newton are too intelligent and original to resign themselves to the rôle of the dead-dog politician, of whom Carlyle spoke as surging up and down the flood by virtue of superior levity, going nowhither, but admired by some for his conspicuous situation. On the other hand, they lack incentive, and rarely acquire that habit of hard work and that insensibility to disappointment and disgust which, more than any extraordinary talent, bring the self-made statesman to great position.

Lord Newton is Lord Rosebery on a smaller scale. He has the same dawdling disposition. He has the same relish in scoring off others, especially if they happen to be his political friends. He has the same intense distaste for being himself scored off. He has, like Lord Rosebery, a good deal of wit, some wisdom, and an excellent style. He has dabbled in many things : in diplomacy, literature, public business, mastiff-breeding, yeomanry tactics. As a writer, an Ambassador, or a Minister, he might easily have won real eminence had he given his not inconsiderable abilities full play. As it is, he is chiefly famous for a few rather flippant speeches, for an excellent Life of Lord Lyons, and some illuminating reflections on diplomacy, for heretical views regarding the dismalness of county cricket, and for routine work in the oversight of British prisoners, which some time ago brought him into a prominence that he appeared to resent.

Into the details of that controversy it is unnecessary to enter. The only indictment to be framed against Lord Newton, and through Lord Newton against the class he represents, concerns the manner rather than the matter of his defence. His lordship was clearly thinking less of the prisoners than of attacks made on himself and his Department. Against the poor halfpennyworth of bread which formed the prisoners' portion in that feast of reason, his apologia in the House of Lords, we had an intolerable deal of sack in which Lord Newton drank his own health, and conveyed complimentary sentiments to his colleagues. All his wit—and on this occasion he hardly did justice to his reputation—was used against " editors and sub-editors," officers released from internment, and other noxious people who dared suggest that Lord Newton might possibly have done better.

Now it is certain that Lord Newton is not a callous man. He is not a stupid man. Probably he is not a particularly egotistical man. He is only displaying with a naïveté rather surprising in one with so decided a sense of humour, the attitude of his caste towards public affairs. It is, I think, an attitude in some ways quite peculiar to this country, and is the natural but singular consequence of the disturbance of the old balance of the Constitution which took place two centuries ago.

In some countries Ministers are still truly the servants of the Crown, and in a very real sense responsible to the monarch. In other countries Ministers are under a constant obligation to satisfy Parliaments, or Parliamentary groups, or Parliamentary Committees. But in England, though some of the Hanoverian monarchs were allowed a most dangerous liberty in foreign affairs, they were not in a position, as the German Emperor is, to call their Ministers to account for every action. On the other hand, while public opinion no doubt rules in England in the long run, the run is often very long indeed. A party returned to power is secure against anything except formal defeat. In theory a Government is constantly under check, liable to dismissal for any indiscretion or misbehaviour; in practice it can look forward to enjoyment of power as long as it likes to stay, short of the full legal term. The minority in Parliament may ask questions, but they need not be answered; it may propose votes of censure, but they are readily defeated. There is really no check on Ministers beyond their consciences, the prejudices of their supporters, and the fear of being beaten at elections. The fact is recognized in Parliamentary terminology.

A Government is said to be "strong" when it has not only a secure majority, but a long period before it. It is said to be "weak," whatever the majority, when a General Election is within measurable distance. Politicians speak of an "exhausted mandate." What they really mean is that a Government nearing the end of its tether must act with a quite accustomed sense of responsibility, and is therefore, in view of its general habits, not likely to act with vigour.

In peace time, when the consequences of failure in office are less manifest, Ministers are generally able to defeat the critic, either by raising new issues or by opposing to him the obedient mass of their voting power. This safety breeds an astonishing indifference to public opinion. But in war, when effect follows cause with startling rapidity, critics, especially out of Parliament, tend to be more severe and more persistent, and party bonds are apt to loosen. Habit, however, persists in the ruling class. Placemen are not less but more hostile to what they regard as interference, and more disposed than usual to resort to the old dodges: "contrary to public interest," "advice of the responsible officials," "need of consulting other interests which cannot be too closely specified," and so forth. Hence the phenomenon, spoken of as if it were something extraordinary, of a Government out of touch with the House of Commons, and a House of Commons out of touch with the country.

Men like Lord Newton especially, men of good family and large possessions, take a view of their responsibilities which is almost humorous in times like these. They conceive themselves as having done a great favour to the nation in emerging from their pleasant country-houses to bear part of the burden and heat of the day. Being well-bred men and patriots, they are not likely to remind the nation of its debt so long as the nation "behaves." But when the nation begins to ask whether they are really doing their duty, this high calm is apt to evaporate in a spluttering indignation. We saw a good deal of the spirit during the Budget fight. " We are a priceless blessing to the nation," said the ruling class in effect, "and are willing to continue so—on our own terms. On any other we propose to make ourselves objectionable."

The steady progress of this anarchic temper in the English ruling classes, following as night the day all attempts to decrease their power, seems natural enough to people who express astonishment at similar phenomena in other countries. That ugly chapter of Ulster, for example, is chiefly remembered as a joke (carried a little too far) by those who find marvellous the action of German-speaking barons in Baltic Russia. We are ready enough to condemn Junkerdom's objection to bear its fair proportion of the burdens of German taxation—an objection which had much to do with the decision for a war of conquest, and had still more to do with the continuance of a war for indemnities. But the Budget revolt could take place without the breath of suspicion being cast on the patriotism of our great landowners. We have been so used in this country to a class which clings stubbornly to privilege, while disclaiming more than the duties it cares to undertake in its own way and for its own profit, and we have been so fortunate thus far in escaping the due pains and penalties for such a state of things, that it is difficult to realize that our own Junker order—polite, pleasant, and liberal-minded in indifferent matters—is in essence quite as class-conscious as Germany's, and much less conscientiously national.

But incidents like that of Lord Newton, arriving together with that extraordinary appeal to the Prussian Order of St. John by our own members of the Order, come as an emphatic reminder of the difference between a true democracy and a bundle of anomalies

like our own State. The nation's passionate interest
in ordinary common Englishmen, simple non-com-
missioned officers and privates, contrasted sharply
with the offended dignity of Lord Newton. The
nation's detestation of the Prussian aristocracy
brought out in strong relief the almost obsequious
approach of the English knights of St. John. The
nation thinks of the Prussian notables who compose
the Order of St. John as ordinary blackguards in an
extraordinary position. But to the princely and noble
British members they are still men of honour who can
be addressed without incongruity by men of honour.
A large part of the nation looks forward to a League
of Nations. It has an uneasy notion that too many
of its hereditary statesmen look backward on the old
International League of Nobs, and hope that the
family party of Europe will not be altogether broken
up by the present misunderstandings.

Of course, no Englishman can view without strong
dislike the breach by Germany of every civilized convention. But there is a world of difference between
the man who regards Germany as having "not always" adhered to the standard code of "sport" and
fair play, and the man who sees no essential difference
between the crimes of decorated Germans and the
murders and dirtiness of vulgar people. The one will
be ready hereafter to receive socially German princes
and counts, though he will no doubt continue to dislike the German people. The other promises himself
that he will forgive the German people on condition
that they get rid of their princes and counts, but on no
other condition. Both may have to compromise, but
the main difference in their present position is fully
visible : the English populace is fighting for the ex-
tinction of Prussianism, and the English ruling class
is fighting for a favourable accommodation with
Prussians whom it expects at no distant date to meet
at the dinner-table. And, as has happened so often in

great matters, the wide, noble, and generous view is
that of the common man, while the narrow, selfish, and
snobbish view is that of the Olympian god, " careless
of mankind," but most mindful of the *Almanach de
Gotha*.

MR. WINSTON CHURCHILL

AT thirty-seven men looked on Mr. Churchill as a
statesman of some achievement. At forty-seven he
is discussed as a politician of considerable promise.

Mr. Churchill's case is perhaps unique. There have
been rises even more rapid. There has probably been
no fall comparable with his which was not final. If
the dramatic proprieties were consulted, this Lucifer
should not hope again. In fact, he is hoping again
and trying again, for all the world as if he were a
Smiles hero. He has served the Crown as Under-
Secretary of State for the Colonies, President of the
Board of Trade, Home Secretary, First Lord of the
Admiralty, Chancellor of the Duchy of Lancaster,
Hussar Colonel, and Minister of Munitions. And
now that he is beginning life again (not from the
bottom, but from the top, or somewhere near it), his
future is debated with something of the curiosity
attaching to some beardless wonder fresh from the
Oxford Union.

In the days when Mr. Lloyd George was Lime-
housing, still more when, on the very eve of the war,
he led an agitation against our bloated armaments,
many believed that Mr. Churchill would some day
play Elisha to Mr. Asquith's Elijah. The reversion
to the Premier's mantle seemed to lie between him
and Sir Edward Grey; and Sir Edward Grey had
little ambition that way, while Mr. Churchill was
understood to be a very Barkis for willingness. There
is every indication that Mr. Churchill had familiarized

himself with the notion of becoming Mr. Asquith's heir, and perhaps, following the rule of young men of great expectations, looked forward with some impatience to the time when that statesman would go to his own, *i.e.*, " another place."

Undeniably Mr. Churchill went into active training for the part. He affected the eye severe, the mind of formal cut, the wise saws and modern instances of responsible maturity. He emphasized in the strongest possible way the contrast between his own moderation and the sansculottism of Mr. Lloyd George. The more violently the latter swung to the left, the more heavily Mr. Churchill leaned to the right. He seemed to enjoy the "Ohs" of the Outhwaites no less than the "Hear, hears" of those who wanted eight and would not wait.

Now and again he used the tones of the strong party man and the sturdy democrat. But he generally preferred to suggest sane Imperialism, defence without defiance, unfrenzied finance, temperate reform, nation before faction. His new austerity never reached a higher pitch than during the Marconi episode. Nothing could be more admirably dramatic than his indignation when called to give evidence before the Committee. How he rated the chairman for taking him away from the King's business about a sordid affair in which he could have no possible interest ! The part, like most of Mr. Churchill's, was perhaps a little overdone, but at any rate he made it quite clear to the public that one Radical Minister at least need not fear cross-examination as to his investments. The advertisement may have been quite unintentional. But it was there, legible as a sky-sign.

It would be interesting to know what ironical memory of that time remained with the Prime Minister when he strained the allegiance of some of his Conservative followers by inviting Mr. Churchill to join his Government as Minister of Munitions. Equally

pleasant would it be to share Mr. Churchill's inmost
thoughts on the subject—and Mr. Asquith's also.
But if we cannot explore these forbidden regions, we
may at least discuss how it happens that Mr. Lloyd
George was able to take this particular form of re-
venge, and how perhaps the best-equipped intellectually of all our younger men of affairs is now watched
with some anxiety in a post for which the modest
abilities of Dr. Addison were considered adequate.

There is no doubt about Mr. Churchill's capacity.
None but a first-rate man could survive so many first-
rate mistakes. Had he not been, despite his reverses,
formidable as an opponent and valuable as a col-
laborator, Mr. Lloyd George would assuredly not
have encountered severe criticism on his behalf. Nor
would Mr. Asquith have thrust him forward from one
great position to another. Some savour of ridicule
must always attach to the very young man who makes
omniscience his foible. Less kindly emotions are
roused by the spectacle of precocious talents for intrigue and that hunger for place and power that shows
most ungracefully in youth. Mr. Churchill upset his
critics' gravity when at twenty-seven he affected the
airs of a political Manfred, weighted with an intolerable burden of care. The bowed shoulders, the
thoughtful frown, the tense manner, contrasting with
the extreme boyishness of his face and figure, belonged to the realm of pure comedy. On the other
hand, it was as unpleasant to mark his hungry egotism
as to watch the greed of a child miser. But even in
those early days, whether one smiled or railed, one
could not dismiss him as an ordinary poser or an
ordinary place-seeker.

If he overplayed the thinker, he did think. If he
was overeager in his bids for office, he had obviously
a right in the auction-room. Little short of a genius
for affairs could have enabled him to take, as his first
essay, under a dummy chief, the real direction of a

Department so important at the time as the Ministry of the Colonies. In fact, Mr. Churchill has genius, and of a quite high order. It is shown in his purely literary work; there is little better in its way than the biography of his father, while his *River War* is altogether excellent. His best speeches are distinguished by a technical quality, a power of luminous exposition, a dignity of phrase, a mastery, a breadth and grasp that one seeks in vain in the Prime Minister's.

Nor is he merely a man of words. The turn of his mind is, indeed, rather towards action, and it is probably in administration that it finds the keenest satisfaction. He has gifts, in short, which might entitle him without presumption to expect the highest position in the State, were they not intermingled with other qualities which make him still, after a life of extraordinary activity, little more than a man of promise.

Perhaps the chief reproach lies with his ancestors. At this distance there is visible in him more than a trace of the termagant humour, the restless levity, and the inordinate vanity of Sarah Jennings. He has the blood also of that Spencer whose name was a byword for unprincipled intrigue in the most unprincipled period in our political history. From the great Duke he inherits, perhaps, his courage, his warlike tastes, much of his intellect, and no little of his facility for espousing new causes and deserting old ones. With John Churchill's steady baseness, cool treachery, and single eye to the main chance, he might easily have rivalled the glory and shame of the founder of his house.

But Mr. Churchill is neither great enough nor bad enough nor narrow enough for that. The American strain in him, mingling oddly with that old English blood, is perhaps responsible for many things. It may have given him a certain impatience for what he

7

once called—while joyously admitting that he had long talked it as a matter of business—"Tory claptrap." It may have imparted an extra touch of recklessness in speculation, while giving him also a doggedness which was not visible in his father, and for want of which Lord Randolph went to pieces after his first defeat. To it may be traceable, more than to any English source, a lack of simplicity, a taste for self-advertisement uncommon in an English aristocrat, an unbridled tendency to naked "bossing" of any "show," and other peculiarities which make Mr. Churchill a difficult man for many plain Englishmen to "get on with."

It is just this failure to get on that lies at the root of the whole mystery of Mr. Churchill's maimed career. He did not get on with the Unionists. After the first raptures he failed to get on with most Liberals. He did not get on with Lord Fisher. It was perhaps not surprising that he did not get on with the Coalition Cabinet as Chancellor of the Duchy—a post for senile wisdom rather than for young pushfulness. Whether the Army did not get on with him, or he with the Army, only he and the Army may say. But the grand gesture with which he went to the trenches was too soon followed by a return to Westminster to suggest entire compatibility.

The whisper goes round that at the Ministry of Munitions Mr. Churchill still fails to get on. His ability is not questioned, but he has that type of masterfulness which irritates while it fails to subdue. Of his relations with the War Cabinet less is said, possibly because there is nothing to say. When the late Lord Salisbury received a suggestion that he should offer a place to Lord Randolph Churchill and thus silence that distinguished outcast's opposition, he replied in parable. "I once had," he said, "a carbuncle on my neck. If I can avoid another I shall do so." The Prime Minister has no such fear of

Lord Randolph's son, and perhaps he is right. It
may be that adversity has taught Mr. Churchill some
lessons which he failed to master in the days of his
facile success.

It would be to the advantage of the country, no
less than of Mr. Churchill, if he could master them.
"For the love of Christ, gentlemen," said Oliver
Cromwell once to the Parliamentarians, "I beseech
you to think it is possible you may be mistaken."
Mr. Churchill's infallibility is one of his chief weaknesses. Taking all knowledge as his province, he
cannot help being superficial, but then every statesman necessarily is that, and it must be said for Mr.
Churchill that he will learn more of a subject in six
months than most politicians do in six years. Unfortunately he will assume that, as soon as he is bored
with learning, there is nothing more to learn, and
will imagine that he is fit to undertake, not merely
the general control which is the business of a political
chief, but the technical ordering of his department.
He goes up in an aeroplane, down in a submarine,
"swots" Mahan and a few textbooks, and considers
himself qualified to be quite other than a Sir Joseph
Porter as Ruler of the King's Navee. Teaching your
grandfather his own business is fully as futile as teaching your grandmother a business less obviously hers.

Mr. Churchill should also learn not to be too much
in a hurry. I have not in mind here those speeches
of his concerning "rats" and "legitimate gambles"
and "victories such as the world has never seen"—
though in each case he would have been wiser to await
the event. I am thinking more of his personal record.
He would have got on faster at a slower pace. He
has been too busy looking after his next job to think
enough of the one in hand. Had he been content
to work steadily and play the game according to the
rules, had he, so to speak, masticated life instead
of wolfing it in great gulps, he would probably have

gone quite as far, without going back at all. But
with him impatience assumes almost the aspect of
nervous disease. He does not know how to wait.
He is a victim of the " Do it now " craze—" it " being
more or less undefined. The sedative influence of
principle he is unhappily denied. Indeed, there is
a good deal of his great ancestor's century in Mr.
Churchill. " Restless, unfixed in principles and place,
in power unpleased, impatient of disgrace," he has
rather close affinity with those brilliant but somewhat
ineffective men whose weaknesses and talents Dryden
has described with such unerring touch in *Absalom
and Achitophel*.

Few men fight successfully against their natures;
and though Mr. Churchill is still young, as statesmen
go, it is probable that time, though it may tame, will
not reform him. It is a pity, for he has the stuff, if
it were not marred, to make a second Chatham, and
half a dozen Pitts. As things are, he is perilously
near a second edition of his father, with just the difference due either to some added tenacity in himself or
some increased tolerance on the part of the public.

MR. HAROLD COX

It is easy to understand why nobody speaks ill of
Mr. Harold Cox. It is not so clear why all men should
conspire with exaggeration to speak well of him.

People of every party think it the proper thing to
pay him the tribute of their usually far from supple
knees. The Liberals reverence him in his quality of
custodian of the Lares of Cobdenism. The Socialists
owe him some tenderness, as a former Fabian, for
what he was, and perhaps for something of what he
still is. The Tories, in opposition at least, respect
him for his quarrels with official Liberalism.

Thus he has won high praise from very different people. I seem to remember words of eulogy from Mr. Balfour. Mr. Asquith once declared him " indispensable" to public life. He received the ominous commendation of Lord Rosebery in a panegyric which would have been a trifle extravagant for Burke. And whenever the Adullamites are gathered together part of their rites is the swinging of a censer before Mr. Cox. After general denunciation of House of Commons decadence and the tyranny of the party machine, Mr. Cox is pretty sure to be mentioned as an example of the kind of man the country wants and cannot get.

It seems to be everybody's business to give Mr. Cox a friendly shove forward. But what is everybody's business is also nobody's. With all this reverence for Mr. Cox no man or party seems fiercely anxious to secure him with hoops of steel. Mr. Asquith found him indispensable, but dispensed with him. Lord Rosebery gave him a character when he could give him nothing else. He rather resembles the village grocer whom the local magnates respect highly, while dealing exclusively with the stores. For him there is always a pleasant "good-morning" and a courteous raising of the whip hand, but the gentry continue to get their currants from town.

There is a reason for everything, and it is not by sheer accident that Mr. Harold Cox has latterly given to the *Edinburgh Review* what everybody agrees was meant for mankind. He belongs, probably, to a class of men noted by Lytton in his slight but suggestive sketch of that forgotten notability, Sir James Mackintosh : " Men who are less valued for any precise thing they have done than according to a vague notion of what they are capable of doing." The quotation may be continued with advantage. "Their powers of comprehension," says the critic, "are greater than their powers either of creation or exposition ; and their energy, though capable of being roused occasionally

to great exertions, can rarely be relied on for any
continued effort. They collect, sometimes in rather a
sauntering manner, an immense store of varied information. The faculty of comprehending genius may
give them, in a certain degree, the power of imitating
it, whilst ambition, interest, and necessity will at times
stimulate them to extraordinary exertions. As writers
they usually lack originality, ease, and power; as men
of action, tact, firmness, and decision. In society,
however, the mere faculty of remembering and comprehending a variety of things is quite sufficient to
obtain a considerable reputation."

It might be added that a common characteristic of
such men is excessive reverence for authority and a
tendency to quote it chiefly in a negative sense.
"There is a Parliament wit," says Halifax, "to be
distinguished from all other kinds; those who have it
do not stuff their heads only with cavils and objections." Closely regarded, "cavils and objections"
are the main stock-in-trade of men like Mr. Cox.
Often the cavils are justified and the objections sound;
Mr. Cox's warnings against profligate expenditure
and unscientific taxation during the present war
might have been profitably heeded by three Chancel-
lors of the Exchequer. But there are limits to the
usefulness of a critic of this kind, and there are occasions when he is not useful at all. It needs no ghost
come from the grave of old systems to tell us, as Mr.
Cox does, that there are many difficulties in the way
of a League of Nations. That everybody knows.
What we want is wise counsel as to how the difficulties
may be overcome.

There is something curiously illuminative in one
little fact of Mr. Cox's early life. He belongs to the
distinctly upper stratum of the middle classes. His
father was a county court judge. I am aware that
county court judges are—or were—counted hardly
human (except in their liability to err) by my lords of

the King's Bench, but ordinary people quite rightly
regard them as personages of considerable dignity and
emolument. Mr. Harold Cox was thus from his cradle
in an atmosphere of refined enlightenment. He imbibed everything in the way of academic culture that
Tonbridge and Jesus College could give him, distinguished himself greatly in mathematics and political
economy, and acted as an Extension Lecturer in the
latter subject.

Then, "in order to gain an insight into the life of
English labourers," he spent a year working as an
agricultural labourer in Kent and Surrey. There is
nothing very extraordinary in this fact. It was a comparatively common thing in the eighties, when social
questions were very much to the fore, for educated
young men to take a turn at manual work with a view
to qualify as "authorities" on such questions. But
it may be suggested that, while this sort of thing may
be very good fun, and capital experience in its way,
the man who embarks solemnly on such an enterprise
in order to "gain an insight" is not to be trusted
with his gains. He will be much farther off reality
when he has finished than before he started.

The only way to understand the poor is to be poor.
There is no tighter freemasonry in this world than
that of those who live on a pound a week or under;
and the coarsest mistakes concerning the manual
worker are those of people who pride themselves on
knowing him through and through. No less reliable
guide exists than the Bishop who boasts that he is
more at home in Canning Town than at Fulham
Palace, or the "social worker" who specializes in
slums. The poor will occasionally be frank with
richer people who approach them naturally; they shut
up like oysters to those who want to study them or to
"do good." After all, it is only natural. An evan-
gelist from Mile End, a cookery expert from Bethnal
Green, or an earnest seeker after social truths from

Wapping, would receive but a cold welcome in
Berkeley Square.

Not that undue stress need be laid on this youthful
adventure. But it does seem relevant to a discussion
of Mr. Cox's mentality. It suggests at once the
lucidity and rigidity of his mind. It would be in-
accurate as well as rude to call it wooden. Let us
rather say it suggests the polish of fine mahogany : it
reflects much light and yet gives none. There is a
certain affinity between Mr. Cox and Mrs. Micawber of
glorious memory. Mr. Cox wanted to get an insight
into labour conditions, and the first thing was to see
the labourer for himself. Mrs. Micawber wanted to
get an insight into the Medway coal trade, and the
first thing was to see the Medway for herself. She saw
the Medway, and little came of it. Mrs. Micawber's
marked logical faculty is also faintly suggestive of
Mr. Cox's. She arranged her major and minor
premises delightfully, and proceeded with resistless
majesty to the syllogism—which generally demon-
strated the impossibility of feeding a man, woman,
and a growing boy (to say nothing of the twins) on
3s. 9d. worth of commission in three months. You
are buoyed up with continual hope that something
practical is going to emerge from this splendid lucidity
—and nothing does. Mr. Cox disappoints in rather
the same way. That beautiful logical mill of his grinds
to perfection, and produces—what ?

The barrenness of Mr. Cox's achievement, as contrasted with the reputation he bears, is perhaps
explained if we understand his as a mind following
generally received ideas rather than its original inspi-
rations. As suggested above, it gives back light, and
does not produce it; it reflects but does not think.
Such minds are seldom fruitful, though they often put
forth an impressive amount of foliage. They also tend
under a great outward show of consistency and calm
reason, to real confusion of thought.

If we examine Mr. Cox's record closely we shall find a sterilizing conflict in fundamentals. He was, as has been noted, a Fabian. That is to say, at one period of his life at least he must have thought himself in favour of the enlargement of the powers of the State to a degree utterly inconsistent with the very root principles of individualist Liberalism. Yet he sat as a Liberal for Preston from 1906 to 1909. Of course an easy explanation is that the Socialistic youth cooled into the moderate Liberal in his progress to ultimate Conservatism, and this theory would seem to gain strength by the clear fact that Mr. Cox is now nearer the right than the left, and that sometimes he even seems a considerable distance from the centre. Occasionally he speaks rather more like a Tory than a disgruntled Whig, and his views on Ireland are hardly distinguishable from Lord Lansdowne's.

But, whatever the case about his Liberalism, it is not easy to square the undoubted fact that he was once a Fabian with the other undoubted fact that he has been a lifelong Free Trader. Free Trade may be a good or bad thing, or it may be sometimes good and sometimes bad. But the very soul of Collectivism is combat, and the very soul of Free Trade is acquiescence. The Collectivist says economic forces must be consciously controlled, or there will be chaos; the Free Trader believes that the only safe plan is full liberty for economic forces to act and react. The Free Trader's attitude to the State resembles that of Artemus Ward to the fire brigade, whom he thanked for "kindly refraining from squirting." The Collectivist would have a constant stream of vivifying interference.

It is, therefore, I think, clear that at one period of his life, at least, Mr. Cox was in a state of confusion on fundamentals—not an uncommon case with young men, and a quite forgivable case with the majority—but rather serious in the special circumstances, for

Mr. Cox's whole position as a teacher is that of *ex cathedra* infallibility. The point of honour must always be considered. You and I might do what is not done at a duke's dinner party, and still hold up our heads as human beings; not so a lifelong professor of good form. The claim of the Coxes is not that they are sometimes very right, but that they are never wrong. And one mistake is fatal to the whole pretension.

I imagine the Free Trader was even at the time more the real Harold Cox than the temporary Fabian. For Free Trade—or more correctly the idea behind Free Trade—is his natural element. To his acute and well-regulated mind the impregnability of the Cobdenic doctrine to purely logical attack would necessarily appeal. It is just as impossible to deny that free exchange, taking a large area, favours the production of wealth, and that protective duties retard it, as it is to deny that plenty of beef and bread, taking the mass of mankind, are more favourable to vigour than a restricted diet. But some men will die of a steak, and some industries—perhaps even some nations—will die of Free Trade. One seems to catch here the murmured reflection " Why keep them from dying ? Is it an advantage to bolster up the clearly inefficient ?" —a remark that at once reminds one that Free Trade is the political equivalent of Darwinism. " Supply and demand," " buy in the cheapest market and sell in the dearest," " natural operation of economic law," " economic tendencies which cannot be resisted ": what is all this but a variant of the survival of the fittest; "fittest" meaning only those who survive? Free Trade and the doctrine of evolution are both deserving of high respect as an explanation of economic and biological phenomena; but it is hardly fanciful to see in the modern extensions of both the secular cousins of Calvinism.

Calvinism of any kind is a dreary creed, and a certain despair is discernible in most of the economists from whom Mr. Cox has sucked inspiration. His own writings reveal much of the cheerful hopelessness—it is not easy to describe the mood—of a school convinced that, while Manchester was very horrible, it was the best we could reasonably look for, and must be borne with stoicism and even satisfaction, pending the "evolution" of better things. The calm with which philosophers of this school discuss "displacement of labour" through the introduction of new methods or the swift decay of old trades affords perhaps the best illustration of what is here meant.

The extreme ability with which Mr. Cox acts as the exponent of Free Trade doctrines may explain the esteem in which he is held by one party. The general good-will to which allusion has been made can only be understood by those who have come in contact with a singularly engaging personality.

VISCOUNT MILNER

When Lord Milner became a member of the War Cabinet the prevalent feeling was vague distrust. His appointment to the War Office was as generally approved, and not merely on the ground that, compared with his lordly predecessor, his intellectual qualities "stick fiery off indeed."

The truth is that the average man strongly suspects Lord Milner in the capacity of spiritual guide; but, in spite of his many failures, retains faith in his talents for administration in matters where political bias is of small account. He feels, too, that the ruthlessness which appears to lie at the core of Lord Milner's character is an asset in his present office. The War Office wants a head. It has never had one since Lord Kitchener's death, and even Kitchener, who was not in 1915 the Kitchener of Omdurman, could not quite master the job. Mr. Lloyd George was simply a picturesque figurehead and Lord Derby an unimpressive one. Lord Milner is qualified to be much more. He has brains and industry. He dislikes incapacity, and is believed to be no respecter of persons.

In some regards he is exceedingly well fitted to deal with that specially British curse—the lenity to well-connected muddlers, which has evoked the bitter sneer that the English will see their best division broken rather than break their worst General. For while he is a man of no family, and has therefore no relatives to consider, Lord Milner is also the last to be impressed by family trees. That is the common fate of English middle-class statesmen as soon as they have reached' the stage when it is considered worth while to flatter them. Lord Milner's intellectual arrogance makes such abasement impossible. Indeed, he would probably enjoy the discomfiture of a fool all the more because he belonged to a caste.

The common respect for Lord Milner as an instrument, as contrasted with the equally common distrust of him as an influence, has, like most popular instincts, a sufficiently rational foundation. The public respect his Prussian efficiency, but are repelled by his Prussian mind. Much malignant and vulgar nonsense has been written about the accident of Lord Milner's German connections. But, while it is absurd to suggest that he has the smallest sympathy in this war with the land with which he has been so closely connected, there is no gainsaying the fact that his mind, like his features, is of a very Prussian cast. Environment has, indeed, toned down the harsher lineaments of the character. Lord Milner is a pleasant man to talk to. He has a real gift of friendship. He is an intelligent and kindly patron of young men of promise; in fact, no part of his character is more amiable than the paternal tenderness which he, a bachelor, well on in the sixties, shows for clever people

very much his juniors. He is not really "reactionary."
He believes in progress as much as any man; he is
farther from the mere Tory than he is from Mr. Sidney
Webb. His patriotism, in its kind, is indisputable.
He has himself laughed at the folly which imputes to
him, "an out-and-out British Imperialist," a divided
allegiance. But in nothing, truly, is his Prussianism
better revealed than in that same "out-and-outness";
nothing more signally illustrates his intellectual and
temperamental affinities to the professors of Welt-
Politik, whom it is now his business to fight.

The old English word for colonies was "planta-
tions," and the idea of a garden still best indicates
what was long the underlying principle of English
colonization. What we call the British Empire is a
gigantic absurdity considered as an Empire; it is a
wonderful thing considered as a natural growth. Our
gardens have occasionally been watered by unjustly
spilled blood; some of them were Naboth's vineyards
wrongfully seized. But in the main they have been
made by the spade and not by the bayonet; they are
the monument of free men and free forces.

The German idea of a colony, on the other hand,
has always been a well-managed factory of raw
material, with everything—more especially the native
and the colonist—put in its right place. Some thirty
years ago the German colonial idea, in the general
worship of German things which followed 1870, began
to gain ground in this country, and Lord Milner must
be credited with his part in that cynical reaction.
Coolly examined, the whole notion of modern Imperialism in its extreme expression is Prussian. The
United Kingdom is to be made as "efficient" a workshop as Germany, a clearing-house and central power-
station, and a pleasure-place for plutocrats from everywhere. The Dominions, too big to be forced, are to
be shepherded into a state of dependence, their
development canalized and stereotyped. The tropical

dependencies are merely to subserve the interests of great British monopolies. The only material difference between the German and the English school is that in Germany aims are discussed frankly and pursued logically, whereas here realities are obscured by sentimental talk, and policy is subject to sharp variations.

About a generation ago South Africa happened to be in a position half-way between the Crown Colonies and the more developed States of Australia and Canada, and to its great misfortune the great gold and diamond discoveries precisely synchronized with the rise of the new eagerness for exploitation on Prussian principles. In the older States foundations were laid by hardworking pioneers, and the edifice was completed by citizens. In South Africa gamblers began the work, and syndicates continued it. There was real danger at one time of a veritable dictatorship by boards of directors. It is due to Lord Milner to note his dislike and hostility to the low men who wished to impose on half a continent the most degrading of all tyrannies. He worked his hardest to transfer practical sovereignty from the Randlords to the British Crown, and in the end he won. His imperialism was not mixed up, like that of even Rhodes, with baser ingredients. He regarded only what he thought the true interests of Britain and Africa. Moreover, he was free from some singular illusions of Rhodes and others. Rhodes shared an error common both to the British Pacifist and the British Imperialist. He acted as if England, by some law of nature, was always safe. The Pacifist thought nobody would ever attack us if we were inoffensive. The Imperialist went a step farther, and could not conceive that even aggression might be risky. The simplicity of the Jameson raid plotters was really more wonderful than their lack of scruple. To Rhodes and his fellows the attempt to subvert the South African Republic was little more than an affair of commercial policy, hardly more important than the despoilment of Lobengula. Their naïve surprise at the noise made by their exploit is truly wonderful in retrospect.

Lord Milner's wider intelligence was capable of no such self-deception. It is true that his judgment has occasionally been deflected by a singular vein of rashness—"damn the consequences" is with him more than the mood of a moment—and in not avoiding the Boer War he committed a capital error; perhaps he had not reckoned on the Victorian War Office. But in a general way he recognized the danger of an adventurous policy unsupported by adequate military force. Hence his anxiety to carry Prussianism to its only logical conclusion, an intense militarism. Lord Milner's enthusiasm for conscription long antedated the present war. For him it seemed mere common sense that strong policy should be supported by strong armaments, and, granting his premises, his conclusions were unquestionably just. Only a people so illogical as the English could at once huzza for " Dr. Jim " and cut down naval and military estimates.

Indeed, such virtue as resides in consistency cannot be denied Lord Milner. His politics are in some senses a little vague. He fits into no English mould. He is in many ways the most lonely figure in our public life. But one principle runs like a rod of steel through his career—a sovereign contempt for the democratic idea. Not that he is in any way kin to the "shoot-'em-down" Conservatives with whom he has been brought into casual association. His model State would tolerate squiredom as little as the walking delegate; for his main quarrel with the democratic idea is that it is inefficient, and his hatred of waste would equally predispose him against a mere gentleman do-nothing caste. He has no manner of use for looking backward to a supposed golden age. He looks eagerly forward to an iron one; his real ideal is Krupp and culture; a highly educated and hardworking upper class, and the masses well fed, well drilled, and broken into contented subordination. And here we arrive at Prussia once more.

The Milner type of mind is tolerably antique. It held, long ago, that man was made for the Sabbath and not the Sabbath for man. It conceives the citizen as existing for the State and not the State for the citizen. And, just as the claims of the individual are nothing beside the claims of the State, so the rights of a great State outweigh those of a small one. The same tidiness of mind which finds individual liberty wasteful and disorderly also deplores the loss of power implied in small nationalities. One can well imagine Lord Milner agreeing with that German professor who saw something positively wicked in the existence of an independent and " slippered " Holland. No doubt the British public has not consciously weighed every act and word of Lord Milner. But it has certainly smelt his essential Prussianism, and has felt with no incertitude his incongruity as a spiritual leader in a war " ostentatiously "—to use the Prime Minister's rather unhappy word—waged in defence of individual liberty and national right.

The strength of this distrust is really an inverted compliment to Lord Milner. He is certainly not alone in his views. But they are held by him with absolute sincerity, and the lover of freedom rightly sees his real enemy in the man who hates freedom on principle, and not because his pocket is affected. Lord Milner inspires fear as a disinterested fanatic, for that is really what he is, with all the coolness of his head and heart. He does not merely object to what fails to fit into his system ; he hates it. And Lord Milner's system is just bureaucracy. He is the civil servant above everything. His dislike of democracy is simply, in the ultimate analysis, the dislike of a civil servant for people who " want to know, you know." Democracy is our old friend Tite Barnacle's ogre " the public " : that public which impudently insists on questioning and criticizing, when it should be content with paying taxes and being managed. It is true that Lord Milner's Civil Service would not be a How Not to Do It Department; it would really work, as it does in Prussia. He would do his duty by the herd. But he damns the public as heartily as he did the consequences.

He has been described by his admirers as "the finest flower of human culture the University of Oxford has produced in our time"—which means that he is quite a well-educated man. On the other hand, he has been accused by his critics of committing more coarse and stupid blunders than any public man of his day. The two extravagances contain a morsel of truth. Lord Milner might be considered a youthful prodigy at Oxford, but one doubts whether his powers attracted much attention at Tübingen. And the very things which we are all agreed were errors would never be thought such in the Wilhelmstrasse. Just as alcohol always retains a flavour of the substance of origin, so Lord Milner is just a little foreign in his strong points and his weaknesses. He is too well educated to retain an instinct. He is too intelligent to be altogether wise. In nothing is he less English than in the splendid confidence with which he steers straight for a wrong conclusion which, by all known rules, should be the right one. His arguments against the grant of self-government to South Africa were really unanswerable; at any rate, they were never answered. Yet "C.-B.," not a very clever man, was right, and Lord Milner, a desperately clever man, was demonstrably wrong.

It is just this want of the homely wisdom of the common Englishman that makes it a little doubtful whether Lord Milner will succeed wholly in his new task. All will be done that a cultivated and strong intelligence, directed by patient industry, can do. But the man who is to make the most of the New Army

8

wants something more than intelligence. He must be able to feel and to smell what is right and what is wrong. And there are two things deficient in Lord Milner, judging by the facts of his career—he has no nose, and not too much heart.

MR. AND MRS. SIDNEY WEBB

THESE twain the Heavens and the Heavies—the Eternal Blue and the Eternal Blue Book—have joined together; let no man put them asunder.

No man with a sense of the fitness of things is likely to try. For here, if anywhere, is the perfect marriage: two minds with but a single set of thoughts, two typewriters that click as one. It is hard to imagine Marshall without Snelgrove, Swan divorced from Edgar; but all that is nothing to the strain of thinking of Beatrice and Sidney Webb as two distinct and unrelated individuals.

There was a time, of course, when it was impossible to speak of them as "the Webbs." The couple were, in fact, of quite mature years when, as far back as 1892, Miss Potter, eighth daughter of a former Great Western chairman, decided on the uncertain co-operative venture called marriage. It was natural that she should be attracted to Sidney Webb. They were both Fabians. They had both a fancy for arid subjects. She had "personally investigated social and industrial conditions," and written much indigestible matter thereon; the authorship of *The Co-operative Movement in Great Britain* already stood to her credit, and her maiden fancy was musing on *The Case for the Factory Acts*. He, on the other hand, after picking up educational scraps from everywhere, including the sandy wastes of Mecklenburg-Schwerin, had wandered from the City to Whitehall, from one Government office to another, and into the London County Council.

A Cockney of Cockneys, sharp as the London sparrow, and mentally as omnivorous, he had from the first gained his special niche in the Fabian movement. He was its Chief of Staff and Minister of Munitions. There were plenty of excellent artillerists, dashing cavalry leaders, shrewd organizers of ambuscades, clever raiders and camouflagers, who won applause, laughter, and—what they prized equally—the alarmed detestation of the comfortable classes. But, far behind the screen of fighting men, sat the pallid, short-sighted strategist, supplying his troops with facts and figures, arguments and plans of campaign. Mr. Webb has never aspired to the limelight; he never goes "over the top"; his place, and he knows it, is twenty-five miles from the front. Hence nine people out of ten, though they have often heard the name, have the dimmest idea of the man; and the tenth person, who does know him, mingles esteem with a slight tincture of distrust.

It was, it may be repeated, natural that these two should come together; yet the completeness of their union is none the less remarkable. In style they have nothing in common. The man might pass at a Socialist conference for a proletarian of any country; the woman's fine profile gives out the flavour of English exclusiveness. Those who know them best say that this facial dissimilarity is indicative of fundamental differences in their outlook. They go the same road for the same end, but from different motives. Mr. Webb has a wholehearted delight in regimentation for its own sake. He would like to see the world docketed, drilled, ordered, regulated—himself and his like, of course, doing the docketing and regulating—because he honestly thinks that the world would be happier and better for such guidance.

Liberty to him simply means anarchy. It is the

cause of all our troubles. Leave a child in a room
without a fireguard and you get only material for an
inquest. Similarly, the ordinary man, with red blood
and troublesome appetites, is sure to go wrong unless
he delivers himself over to the direction of the brainy,
who alone are to be trusted. It is a friendly instinct,
mingled with a passion for ruled columns and decimal
points, that leads Mr. Webb to his position, and, if
only men and women were without souls, no system
could be better than his.

Unfortunately, they have tastes as well as stomachs,
passions as well as appetites, tendencies to love,
quarrel, and gamble, as well as to work and eat. It is
these uneconomic proclivities that fill Mr. Webb with
gentle disapproval. It is, for example, highly irrational, from his point of view, that the German
should go to his death singing " Deutschland über
Alles," but even more irrational that the Frenchman
should have contributed to that German's mania by
resenting for the best part of fifty years the inclusion
of Alsace-Lorraine in the German Empire. On the
Webb plan there would have been no " Revanche "
trouble. For life, after all, is a question of wages,
doctoring, police, lamp-posts, post-offices, and efficient
sanitation. So long as men work and barter in peace,
are taxed with something like equality, and are disposed of scientifically when dead, what more can they
properly ask? Now, German doctors, police, lamp-
posts, post-offices, and drains are demonstrably as
good as French, and probably there are now very many
more of all these blessings—especially police—in
Alsace-Lorraine than there were in 1870. Why, then,
worry over the childish business of one tricolour or
another? It is pure unreason on both sides. Let us
have more reason, says Mr. Webb, and if reason is
incompatible with human nature, let us get rid of
human nature. We shall be much better without it.

Mrs. Webb, on her side, is credited with a rather

severer basis for her views. She believes in shep-
herding the masses not so much because they are
foolish as because they are desperately wicked. She
distrusts the natural man, just as she distrusts the
untutored mother. The latter will probably feed her
baby (which she should never have had, and would
not have had but for the gross neglect of eugenic
science) on porter and chipped potatoes. The former
will indulge, if he gets the chance, certainly in pitch-
and-toss, and quite possibly in manslaughter. Look
at the statistics. And there follows the dismal family
history of Ann Veronica Patterson, married in 1814,
whose 483 descendants have wallowed in every kind
of infamy, and have cost the ratepayers and taxpayers
£83,359 18s. 6½d. Also the beneficial effect of State
Socialism in East Prussia, where parents are allowed
no choice in regard to the future of their offspring—
a joint committee of schoolmasters, professors, em-
ployers, and Civil Service officials deciding what
trades the children shall follow when they have
reached the age of fourteen. Mrs. Webb never
changes. It is believed she discusses Reconstruction
in bed when air-raids banish sleep. It is certain that
she quelled the nervousness of her maids by getting
them insured, and showing them the smallness of the
premium. How could they harbour panic when
trained statisticians estimate the betting at more than
4,000 to 1!

The Webbs might have been compounded out of
half a dozen Dickens characters. There is a good
deal of Gradgrind in them—"facts, facts, give me
facts." Their investigations into foreign affairs
rather recall the methods of Count Smorltork. They
have something of Miss Rosa Dartle's habit of getting
information and extracting admissions, under the
cloak of an enormous and quite fictitious innocence.
They toss the ball from one to the other with all the
skill of Mrs. Heep and her son. And in other ways

they suggest the philanthropists of *Bleak House*. True, 41, Grosvenor Road, where Mr. and Mrs. Webb sometimes give modest dinners to very great people, is as different as can be, in its ordered neatness, from the dingy den in Thavies Inn whence Mrs. Jellyby directed her African projects. Yet there is a certain flavour of Borriaboola-gha in the Webb activities. The white man is a hobby to them as the black man was to Mrs. Jellyby. They have an affinity for all other people with missions, as she had. Secretaries get in the soup, and Blue Books into the conversation. There is a general flavour of paper in the entrées and of red ink in the claret, excellent as it may be. When an unrepentantly human being gets in that company he begins to understand why the Girondists had such short shrift, why the "intellectual" everywhere, while he helps to promote revolutions, is the first to suffer from them. Mere despair of arguing with people who do not argue in return, but only refer you to what the Actuary-General of Friendly Societies said in 1872, makes one want to knock this modestly assured omniscience on the head.

The Webbs are Girondists. One may almost call them the English Rolands. True, they are not "out" for anything dramatic in the revolutionary way; and if Mrs. Webb had to mount the scaffold, her last words would probably be statistical. Nor can one figure Mr. Webb, however disconsolate, throwing himself on the point of his sword; the sword is not in his line. But the pair are, all the same, playing something the same part the Rolands played. They have done much to create the Mountain, and they are already distrusted by it. I have heard that Messrs. Chesterton and Belloc were at one time under the fascination of the Webbs, just as Robespierre yielded to that of the Rolands; to-day they are already playing with their snickersnees.

Nor does the rank and file of "Labour" altogether

trust or like the Webbs. They draw up the "settle-
ments of the European map," "programmes of industrial reconstruction," and the rest of it, because they
can hardly be dispensed with. After all, a party
pretending to domination must make some show of
understanding the larger questions of the day. The
Webbs at least give rational form to these aspirations.
They can invest most proposals with plausibility.
It is only natural that their general attitude at this
time should rather repel the simple-minded patriot,
who forgets that the Webbs, in the Minority Report
on the Poor Laws, did fight on the side of the angels.
But they are wholly sincere and disinterested. They
are in no sense hypocrites, or even fanatics, except as
an asylum warder may be fanatical against strong
delusion. They look on this war as on any other
form of waste, as pure madness, and they want to
place the world in a strait waistcoat. Is it their
fault that the straitest of all strait waistcoats are made
in Germany?

That, of course, is the whole secret of the sleepless
suspicion with which this amiable couple are watched
in many quarters to-day. The social system they
stand for has largely been realized by one State.
Germany has gone farther along the Webb route than
any other nation. In the rebound against all German things it is natural, even if unreasonable, that
all apostles of regimentation should incur some degree
of depreciation. Before the war Webbism had begun
to be a weariness. It is now perhaps viewed with a
more positive dislike.

GENERAL SMUTS

THERE are two men who most nearly express the
inarticulate heart of half--and that not the least intelligent half—of the English people. And neither of
these men is English. One is the exceedingly powerful personage who speaks for the American people.
The other is the South African Dutch barrister who
eighteen years ago took the field against us under
Delarey.

The fact, superficially surprising, is capable of
ready explanation. President Wilson and General
Jan Christian Smuts represent things which the great
dumb England has really had in mind during decades
of Whig-and-Tory, Imperialist-and-Little-Englander
nonsense. In the past we have had to choose,
broadly, between undiluted Outhwaite and Lansdowne neat; and now, somewhat to our astonishment,
we find the two not so far from each other, and very
far from us.

It was said of the French Revolution that the
actors were pigmies on the most colossal stage ever
set by fate. That is far truer of the present drama.
In eighteenth-century France, if the men were small,
their ideas were not. In the England of 1918 our
little men are rather bigger than their thoughts and
words. Mr. Asquith has often spoken with a grave
eloquence worthy of the times. Mr. Lloyd George
has coined one or two phrases of pure gold among a
barrowload of pinchbeck tokens. But the ludicrous
" business as usual " catchwords have predominated,
and, on the whole, our public men recall the players
in the wood near Athens. We know that Pyramus
is really Bully Bottom, that the British lion is one
Snug the joiner, that all of them " sweat for bread
upon Athenian stalls " instead of being really the

great of the earth. We feel, too, that they are dreadfully afraid of being hanged, "every mother's son," should they play the part too convincingly.

Small wonder, indeed, that the mere politician should be a little confounded by the portents of these times! For he is most ignorant of what he should be most assured. He knows nothing of Europe, and almost nothing of his own people—less than nothing (since Mr. Kipling is his main interpreter) of those English-speaking peoples who belong to what we call the "Empire."

Some two generations ago England made up its mind that it did not belong to the European system. Its attitude to Continental questions is well expressed by Carlyle: "Tumble and rage, ye rotten waifs and wrecks (the great States of Europe); clash and collide as seems fittest to you; and smite each other into annihilation at your good pleasure." There was a time when this nonsense at least sounded sublime, when it suggested splendid strength and self-sufficiency. But in reality our magnificent isolation was simply a rather undignified sleeping partnership with Prussia. In practice our indifference to European problems resolved itself into thanking Heaven that Bismarck and William I. were pious men and good husbands, and relying on them to trounce France whenever she should need it. Meanwhile we would go on with our civilizing mission in the wild places of the earth. We would be a Colonial Power, a Mohammedan Power, any kind of Power but a European Power. As such we could have no kind of collision with the Teutonic cousin—the "whale and the elephant" would never fight a duel—and we could make our money in peace.

It is not easy, however, to think in watertight compartments. After some decades of pro-Prussianism in foreign politics we began to "think Imperially" after the Potsdam manner. Mr. Kipling was the

Aaron of British Prussianism, and Joseph Chamberlain its Moses; both showed extreme toleration of the golden-calf worship of Rhodes and the Randlords, which, indeed, was in no sense incongruous with their Imperial creed. Mr. Chamberlain's scheme was wholly Prussian as far as it went. True, he proposed to employ silken chains instead of the heavy fetters of militarism; but the object was to restrict, canalize, and stereotype in the true Prussian way. Canada was to be the granary and lumber-store of the Empire; South Africa its mine and vineyard; Australia its wool farm. On the other hand, Great Britain was to serve the Dominions as workshop, drawing-room, and park. In the pleasant southern counties and the Scottish deer-forests the plutocrats of industrial England and the grain and meat kings, the diamond and gold millionaires of the Oversea States, were to hold sway over a meek, dependent race; in the grimy North and Midlands and the spoiled valleys of Wales a breed of rough helots, content with slightly dearer food on account of certain wages improvements worked out to the farthing's-worth, would perennially labour in order to supply Greater Britain with all it needed in the way of machinery and manufactured stuffs.

There was no thought in all this of the principle to which we now do at least lip service—the principle of nationality. Eternal tadpolism was the vision for the Empire; eternal helotry for the Mother Country. There was no thought that Australia, South Africa, Canada, or New Zealand might conceivably like to grow up in their own way; that they might wish to evolve their own foreign policy, their own arts, their own standards of taste, their own scheme of life in every direction—in a word, that they might want to be nations. We may call it pure Prussianism, if we divest Prussianism for the moment of the quite incidental association of barbarous cruelty. Prussia

is capable of vileness and brutality astonishing to
the modern Englishman, but she is not gratuitously
bloodthirsty; she only wades through slaughter to
an ideal. She would, no doubt, if she got her way,
strive faithfully to make Poland richer, more produc-
tive, and even (in the lowest material sense) happier,
than ever before. The one thing she will not do
willingly is to permit Poland to develop on Poland's
own lines, and it was precisely such liberty that
Chamberlain's scheme forbade to the British
Dominions.

The Kipling-Chamberlain view, so far as it holds
to-day, is a real danger to what we call the British
Empire, but what General Smuts (as we ought to
note carefully) prefers to call the British Commonwealth. If we go on thinking All-Red, if we imagine
that "Imperial sentiment" is to be fostered by toss-
ing a few trumpery peerages and orders across the
seas, if we conceive of the "daughter States" as a
mob of barges to be towed wherever the Mother
Country steam tug cares to drag them, our mistake
will be fatal. These young communities are not
fighting for Britain or "the Empire," but for their
own menaced nationhood. They are having a dreadful tussle to withstand Prussianism in shining armour.
They will not voluntarily abase themselves before
Prussianism in pantomime properties.

Read with discernment, the speeches of General
Smuts will be found to contain more than one hint on
this point. Of his loyalty there is as little doubt as
of his penetrating intelligence. The first has been
proved by deeds which are already great history.
The latter has been illustrated in the astonishingly
varied successes of a man yet less than forty-eight.
When Smuts was a mere lad, son of a farmer in Cape
Colony, the attention of Cecil Rhodes, among whose
virtues the capacity to discern and the will to assist
native ability were conspicuous, was turned to his

great powers of mind. The Dutch stripling was given every chance, and fully availed himself of his opportunities. At Cambridge he took a double first in the Law Tripos; he fought brilliantly during the Boer War; he played an influential part in the peace negotiations; as a Minister he applied himself, when the Constitution was granted, to the work of national reconstruction and racial conciliation; he shares with Botha the credit of quelling the rebellion of De Wet and Beyers; and he broke the back of the German resistance in British East Africa. Perhaps we must go back to Clive before we find, in the case of a man not bred to arms, so complete a union of the talents of the soldier and the administrator.

But there is a certain coldness and hardness, as of the diamond, in all this brilliance. That General Smuts is a humane man we know from every action of his life. There was no mistaking the genuineness of his emotion when he reluctantly declared for an aerial reprisal policy against Germany on the grounds of military necessity. But it needs only one glance at the high forehead, the steely eyes, the straight eyebrows depressed in an habitual half-frown, the emphatic nose, the tightly closed lips, and the gigantic chin to beware of trusting to any human weakness deflecting the deliberate judgment of his intelligence. He is a type altogether un-English, innocent of English double vision and compromise; he understands nothing of partly circular triangles and "liberal oligarchies." His mind is perhaps as clear of cant as any living man's, while most Englishmen clothe themselves in cant as in a garment.

This must be remembered in assessing the loyalty of General Smuts. It is not loyalty to a King-Emperor. It is still less loyalty to Downing Street, Park Lane, or Berkeley Square. It is loyalty to a country and to an idea, not to an "Empire." Smuts's country is South Africa; his idea is demo-

cracy : the rule of the people, and not the rule of
any section of the people, be it "Labour" or some
other. And his "democracy" is no molluscoid
organism fit only to exist in a world of molluscs.
He is for a League of Nations, but he means it to
be something very different from an International
Band of Unfulfilled Hope. For him democracy is
indeed the rule of peace, but a rule potentially terrible
to the enemies of peace.

And it is clear that, while willing enough to help
the old world to throw off its fetters, he looks with
greatest hope to the new world. His piercing intelligence was the first to recognize the immense difference brought about by President Wilson's decision to
enter the war. To-day he, above all other statesmen,
realizes that this is no dynastic struggle to be patched
up by another Berlin or Vienna conference, but a
life-and-death fight between two principles. The old
world lived in a state of unstable equilibrium, and
the collapse was bound to come. A jumble of pure
autocracies, mixed constitutions, related dynasties,
scheming kings, insincere diplomacies, in Europe; a
rotting anarchy of dying systems in Asia; weakly
violent Governments and dangerously rich territories
in South America; and elsewhere young communities
in moral and intellectual habit far more remote from
the aristocracy-hidden European than the Prussian is
from the Japanese—how could such a chaos subsist
indefinitely? Germany's enterprise, properly understood, was to give the world the uniformity of an
efficient rule from above. She wanted to be a new
Rome, giving law to the world as Rome did, but
perhaps, like Rome, not unwilling to learn from her
captives. The German sense of tidiness was affronted
by the disorderly arrangements of the old world; the
German sense of thrift rebelled against the spectacle
of competing armaments, pegged-out and undeveloped
claims, and unemployed resources. We shall wholly

misunderstand the philosophical basis of pan-Germanism if we fail to recognize a certain inhuman grandeur in the conception of a whole world as well ordered, as well developed, and as well disciplined as the great Hohenzollern farm which we call the German Empire.

And it is still the question to-day whether the German idea shall prevail or another the world has still to test. There can be no question of *status quo*. There must be the symmetry of freedom or the symmetry of a triumphant tyranny. Despotism must conquer or be conquered, now and by present weapons, or later, and with still more frightful means. We must all be slaves or all be free. General Smuts has happily decided that we must all be free; one shudders at the thought of what might have happened had his mind been captivated by the other ideal, which now, as in Napoleon's time, satisfies many brilliant intellects. But let us not fail to draw the correct inference. The British Monarchy need not share in the fall of other venerable thrones; but the British Empire must become the British Commonwealth. The new Poland must be paralleled by a new Ireland; there must be free co-operation everywhere or frank divorce; there must be no attempt to treat the Dominions as mere pawns in the game of European politics. With the British people General Smuts is ready to make common cause; but does he quite identify the British people with the British ruling class? What virtually amounted to the assertion by General Smuts of a Monroe Doctrine for South Africa passed almost unnoticed; it was in reality a most important declaration, and one to be well pondered by our statesmen. It laid down the principle that the Dominions are nations, and that the pressure of the heel of a single European soldier in white man's Africa will be resented just as we should resent the presence of a foreign garrison in the Isle of Wight. The statement has implications which deserve close consideration.

It may be an exaggeration to say that General Smuts was included in the War Cabinet in order to reassure the British people. But it is certain that his inclusion has had that effect; the public mind accepted him as a counterpoise to elements it distrusted wholly. This is the more remarkable because a certain shadow of suspicion once rested on the General. Labour had not forgotten his part in the suppression of the Syndicalist strikes in Johannesburg. In more exalted circles there may have lingered doubts based on his enigmatic character. How he is now regarded by the thoroughgoing Imperialist is uncertain. But the British people, always wiser than its rulers, looks to him rather than to some of its own race for the right word. More than once the War Cabinet has taken shelter behind the prestige of his name; it will be wise to mark with understanding and without resentment the slight suggestion of warning which lies behind some of his utterances.

General Smuts may be relied on to do his best for Great Britain, however foolish, as against Germany. But he is not necessarily allied for ever to British Imperialism. At the risk of being wearisome, it may be well to point out once more that he has frequently said he prefers the words "British Commonwealth" to the words "British Empire." It may be that General Smuts is a fanatic for fine shades of meaning, like that Sir James Mackintosh who debated for six months whether he should say "utility" or "usefulness," and changed the ideas of a lifetime after half an hour's conversation with Pitt.

It may be. But most people, after a quite insignificant personal contact with General Smuts, would say that he is not quite that kind of man.

MR. ARTHUR HENDERSON

HE used to be called "Uncle Arthur" by the fellow trade unionists. Perhaps he still is, the "Right Honourable" notwithstanding. For the nickname is too good an inspiration to be lost. There is something richly avuncular in Mr. Henderson. He is too young and vigorous to be grandfatherly, far too dignified to become mere "mate," too sympathetic to be without a familiar appellative.

"Uncle" exactly suits him in his capacity of Labour leader. He smiles at an audience as if he had just tipped each individual member of it, and in such sort as to suggest a pocket still bulging with sixpences. He has the weight of experience, as an uncle should, but all an uncle's tolerance for the pranks of youth. "Boys will be boys, but when you're as old as I am——" and then follows the sageness of counsel which fails to offend. How could it, with that good-humoured face, innocent of all irony, that well-groomed, prosperous figure, and that heavy watch-chain, all telling of the battle of life well won?

A comfortable man is Mr. Henderson. He belongs to the "aristocracy of Labour." He has worked with his hands—he was apprenticed as a moulder on Tyneside—but it was long, long ago. He has been in trade union work these many years. He has brought up a family on it, and three of his sons have done their duty as soldiers in the war. He got into Parliament through it some fourteen years ago, winning Barnard Castle (which he still holds) in a three-cornered contest. Since then he has been at the very heart of the Parliamentary Labour movement, and now seems almost to enjoy the freehold of its chairmanship. He has found time for civic activities; he has never ceased to be a local preacher of the

Wesleyan persuasion, and at Bands of Hope, Pleasant Sunday Afternoons, and the like he is an honoured figure. All this experience has given him a gift of pontifical speech, a considerable knowledge of many things, a practical faculty in public business. It has helped to give him also a certain very British woolliness of mind, which explains much in his recent career.

I remember reading a speech by Mr. Henderson very early in the war. He stated that he first had his doubts as to the wisdom and justice of our refusal to remain neutral, but after spending a whole Sunday afternoon reading the British Blue Book he came to the conclusion that war was justified and indeed inevitable. That is very typical of the man. Words convinced where deeds did not. He was not going to condemn the tiger because he saw it actually rending a lamb; that might be unjust to the tiger. But he could not resist affidavits from the official shepherds and an authoritative zoologist from South Kensington.

It is, of course, the more to Mr. Henderson's credit that, being thus constituted, he did, in fact, after accepting the evidence, accept also the logical consequences of his conversion. He drew apart from the Keir Hardies and MacDonalds. A pacifist by nature and habit, he threw himself energetically into war work, and the value of his influence in those early days can hardly be overstated. His honesty is unimpeachable. But the story of this particular pleasant Sunday afternoon is none the less significant. In case of an escape of gas one trusts the man with a nose rather than the man who looks up *Sanitary Hints for Householders*. Mr. Henderson had no nose for Junker Germany. The fact makes one wonde. whether he has a nose for many other things.

He certainly had none for revolutionary Russia. He is not to be blamed for the failure of his mission. It was bound to fail. Apart from the *damnosa hereditas*

9

of Lord Milner's junketings with the Stürmers and Protopopoffs, every circumstance conspired to make impossible Mr. Henderson's task of People's Ambassador to the triumphant proletariat. He was sent out by a Cabinet quite undecided whether to welcome or reprobate the revolution. Among his credentials was that extraordinary speech of congratulation by Mr. Bonar Law which was half dirge and half insult. He knew no word of any language but his North-Country English. His Socialism was destitute of any philosophical basis. The whole habit of his mind was bourgeois. He knew the British Labour movement through and through, and this knowledge at least served him well in contact with the Petrograd zealots. For when they began to quote that Bible of Collectivism, *Das Kapital,* of Karl Marx, Mr. Henderson could always deftly turn the conversation to practical trade union organization, of which his hosts were abysmally ignorant.

Mr. Henderson thus retained a certain personal prestige. But in that whirlpool of conflicting tendencies, among the Girondins, the ferocious logicians of the Extreme Left, the interested schemers, the cosmopolitan spies, and the mere miscellaneous blackguards with whom the Russian capital swarmed, it was impossible for him either to control or divine tendencies. He could only judge things by their names, and the same names mean very different things in different countries. Mr. Henderson was misled, and he misled his chief when he returned.

We do not know the complete history of the Stockholm Conference. But there is every reason to believe that the Prime Minister coquetted with the idea for some time before he threw it over, and, with it, Mr. Henderson. A Minister can hardly be retained in a Cabinet which decisively rejects his views on a vital question. The ejection was inevitable, but it was a right instinct which protested against the manner of it. It was felt that Lord Curzon would not have been treated in that particular way. The " doormat " incident was resented by thousands who had little sympathy with Mr. Henderson's views. That it has rankled with its victim there can be little doubt; probably wounded self-pride has thrown him considerably more to the left than he would otherwise have gone. He is not a little vain; a certain pliability mingles with some stubbornness in his character, and there are clever people not slow to take advantage of these weaknesses.

Mr. Henderson, the least sphinx-like of figures, remains rather an enigma. He is busily, and with some success, building up a new party organization. Is it a case of " Sic vos non vobis "? Will he use the instrument himself, or is it being prepared for another? And if he is to be the leader, what lead will he give? Certainly no politician has a larger opportunity. A great political genius, with no point of view but that of the architect, would prefer his materials to any at present available. He could be sure of a great and fairly permanent majority. He might have with him the men who do the best work with their hands and those who do the best work with their brains. He could settle for ever problems soluble by no other formula. He might make us democratic without vulgarizing us still further. He might preserve all that is useful and dignified in the remains of aristocracy, while calling into life a whole world of new energies. He might make of our lopsided country, with its starved land and overgrown towns, its contrasting superfluity and indigence, a thing of health and symmetry—not the " workshop of the world," or its counting-house, or a millionaires' pleasure-garden, but the home of a sanely developed race.

But though England is inclined to democracy, England is by no means disposed to the rule of mere

"Labour." It was probably never less inclined for experiments of the Russian kind. It is not going simply to swap oligarchies, and it thinks, with some reason, that a purely Labour oligarchy would be probably the worst of all oligarchies. Besides, Mr. Henderson, the product of the chapel and the trade union, with little intellectual energy, and an overplus of Victorian primness, is hardly the man one figures either as the chief of a faction or the leader of a nation. In the whole Labour Party, indeed, there is no evidence of a mind capacious enough for the work of social and political reconstruction on broadly democratic lines. It is much more probable that the work Mr. Henderson is doing will be completed by some quite unknown person now in a trench in Flanders or Artois. And probably that person will be either a poor man of family or a true sansculotte.

It is, after all, seldom that one of Mr. Henderson's type successfully guides any great movement. Small respectability is at a disadvantage in appealing to the masses in times of great exaltation. It knows men neither at their best nor at their worst. It is without either the intuition of genius or the sympathy born of experience. Great popular leaders generally come from above or from the very depths. I think it was Lamb who remarked that while no sense of fitness is outraged by the King's marriage with the beggar maid, we should resent a Royal wedding with the grocer's daughter as bride.

And Mr. Henderson belongs rather to the grocer scheme of things. His abilities and virtues are all on the back-parlour scale. His nose is not to be trusted, as we have seen, and his eyes are by no means "double million gas microscopes of hextra power." He is shrewd in a Sancho Panza way, and by no means deficient in judgment where his own interest is concerned. He is ambitious, too, and in quiet times aspiring and unresting mediocrity often wins the race against great talent. But the present emergency demands a very extraordinary man, and Mr. Henderson is rather a quite ordinary man in a very extraordinary situation.

MR. HORATIO BOTTOMLEY

APPEARANCES notwithstanding, it is a mistake to think of Mr. Horatio Bottomley as a twentieth-century Englishman. He belongs to all ages and all countries, and to a good many limited liability companies.

There is nothing so enduring as the ephemeral. Creatures which are born and die within the limits of a summer day came into the world countless ages before the diplodocus, and will gyrate countless ages after man and all his works have disappeared. And in human things nothing is quite so ancient as extreme modernity. The man who above all others seems to belong to the hour, in reality belongs beyond all others to the ages. Pascal and Augustine might find a difficulty in understanding each other; Beau Brummel and one of Juvenal's dandies would have none.

I have not the advantage of Mr. Bottomley's acquaintance. For any knowledge of him I am indebted to newspapers and popular rumour, and to the evidence of his writings and speeches. I did not know, until I turned to a reference book, that he lives in Pall Mall (in company with a stuffed racehorse), and that he has a country place extraordinarily and yet somehow appropriately called "The Dicker." Of his "large financial undertakings in the City," of the part that he played as "pioneer of West Australian mining," I know exceedingly little. I remember vaguely something about the Hansard Union, and more vividly two cases of Regina *versus* Bottomley and Rex *versus* Bottomley, in which the defendant was complimented by his judges on the success with which he conducted his own defence. I have watched Mr. Bottomley in the House of Commons as an Independent Liberal, and I have heard of him on the Turf.

A slight qualification, this must seem, for the task in hand, and, curiously enough, little help comes from the professional biographer, who is a little vague just where one's curiosity is most deeply stirred. Yet I think I know Mr. Bottomley exceedingly well. I have never met him at Pall Mall or "The Dicker," but I perfectly remember him in Revolutionary Paris. I seem to remember also a Mr. Bottomley who called himself something else in the time of good King George. There was a Mr. Bottomley, sometimes Cavalier and sometimes Roundhead, in Stuart England. And I distinctly recall Mr. Bottomley when he shouted for a Business Emperor in fourth-century Rome, and for a Business Consul five hundred years before. He was active at the time of the Punic War, and never more indefatigable than when he led the shout in Athens of " Down with Aristides and the Old Gang." Whether it was the same Mr. Bottomley whose cymbal was loudest over the fall of Pharaoh's army, and whose criticisms were harshest of the Mosaic commissariat and water supply, I cannot definitely say. But it was certainly one of the family.

It is only by thus tracing Mr. Bottomley through the ages that we arrive at the secret of his influence to-day. Mr. Bottomley is always with us; he has conducted his financial operations in talents, sesterces, ducats, pieces-of-eight, and probably in cowrie shells; he has been a pioneer (though not of the pick and spade kind) in Ophir and Golconda as well as Western Australia; he has told people in every dialect what people like to hear. But, just as the ever-present germ is only noticed in conditions favourable to an epidemic, so Mr. Bottomley only becomes important in times of great and rather unhealthy excitement. Carlyle has pointed out that the sceptical ages are always the most credulous because they are the least wholesome. It is certainly true that there is a credulity of unbelief as well as a credulity of faith; that a certain class of practitioner flourishes on overknowingness rather than on simple ignorance.

They that are whole need not a physician, but they that are sick. And the sicker a certain kind of man becomes the more he delivers himself over to the sort of physician who is coldly viewed in Harley Street. "Cure guaranteed" is so much more cheering a formula than "Wait and see." It is pleasing to be told that you will eat your Christmas dinner in peace and comfort; it may even do you good in certain circumstances. You may smile at Blinkum's Pills when you are well, you may scoff at the Something Electro-Magnetic Knee Belt when you have never known rheumatism. But if you really feel ill, and have no faith in doctors, it is quite probable that you will succumb to the wizardry of the irregular practitioner.

When the British nation felt easy in body and mind it treated Mr. Bottomley as the healthy man treats the patent medicine advertiser—as one of the stock jokes of the day. It had, as a whole, small interest in his financial undertakings, just as the newspaper reader cares nothing about the money side of "Life Pellets, Limited," or about the ultimate effect of that company's products on the agonized young typist to whom they are alleged to have brought instant relief. The public did not take Mr. Bottomley very seriously, either as a pioneer of mining or a politician. But it was amused by his talk and rather admired his undoubted cleverness. There was more than one moment when the case appeared to be "Bottomley *contra* Mundum," and Bottomley always won. It was said of Liberty Wilkes that you might strip him, stab him, shoot him, throw him over London Bridge, and next morning he would turn up with a cocked hat, a smart coat, ruffled cuffs, a gold watch in his fob, and a hundred guineas in his pocket. To this irrepressibility much of his popularity was due; the British public admires "gameness" above everything else. The illustration is arbitrary. Mr. Bottomley in no way suggests Wilkes, save in this single particular of winning sympathy that has no kinship to approbation. He excited in his salad days the same sort of interest men show in the patter of a clever cheap-jack at a fair. One may have a shrewd guess that the silver English lever jewelled in eighty-seven holes is not good value for twenty-nine and six; one knows quite well that honest Hodge has no money to waste on such a thing; but the laugh is always against Hodge and with the dashing salesman when the lot is knocked down and Hodge's wife begins to scold him.

Of Mr. Bottomley's cleverness there can be no doubt whatever; he has no intellect in the higher sense, but in brain power of a certain kind he has probably but one living equal. He has a perfect understanding of the common man of a not too pleasant type, who plays "darts" in public-houses and makes a book in sixpences, and sees all life through the gin-dimmed windows of a bar. I imagine Mr. Tittlebat Titmouse, when still a draper's assistant, would have considered "John Bull" prime, and when he arrived at his "ten thousand a year" would have got Mr. Bottomley to write his election address. Mr. Bottomley possesses that kind of frankness that makes an excessive appeal to men who judge all corn by their own mean little private bushels. The more generous world, too, is so used to high professions and low performances, that when a man says, "I pretend to be no better than I am," it is apt to believe that he is much better than he pretends. The saint who steps forth to whip hypocrisy is handicapped first by the suspicion that he may not be a saint after all, and next by the assumption that if he is really a saint his judgment of average humanity will be faulty. But there is always a sympathetic hearing for the man who begins : "You all know me, and I couldn't humbug you even if I wanted to." Mr. Bottomley stands, in the popular eye, for " no humbug " and anti-Puritanism, and that is really the secret of such influence as he possesses.

It would be unjust to Mr. Bottomley to deny that that influence has on the whole been exercised in the right direction during the war. It is probably not very great; though a high value seems to be put on his services as a propagandist, if one can judge from the accounts of a local meeting held the other day. Mr. Bottomley is a patriot in his way; and it is credibly stated that his religious convictions have ripened during the war. Some rhapsodies of his have been the delight of the wicked and the astonishment of the serious, but they are said to represent the author's feeling—at the time. His championship of the under-dogs is equally sincere; he loves to make the widow's heart to sing for joy, and is unquestionably a good-natured man.

But when all allowance is made, it must be said that he is a queer figure for a national hero. In the words of the sage of Chelsea, if he is to be so regarded, then England is " dreadfully off for demi-gods."

THE MARQUESS OF LANSDOWNE

"It hath been an opinion that the French are wiser than they seem, and the Spaniards seem wiser than they are ; but howsoever it be between nations, certainly it is so between man and man ; for, as the Apostle saith of godliness, ' Having a show of godliness, but denying the power thereof,' so certainly there are, in points of wisdom and sufficiency, they that do nothing or little, very solemnly. . . . Generally such (seeming wise) men in all deliberations, find ease to be of the negative side, and affect a credit to object and foretell difficulties."—BACON.

HENRY CHARLES KEITH PETTY-FITZMAURICE, fifth Marquess of Lansdowne, is partly French in blood, but inclined intellectually to the Spaniard as Bacon describes him. Of "seeming wise" men he is perhaps the best example extant. He has done nothing or little, but in such solemn sort that even those who least regard him deem it decent to pay a tribute to his ripe experience, his distinguished talents, his mellow judgment, and the rest of it.

It is only when one looks at all this pomp and prestige with half-shut eyes, resolute not to be blinded by any "property" sun, that one finds how negative the real man is. At "objecting and foretelling difficulties" he has no fellow; but one looks in vain for guidance of the positive sort. Lord Lansdowne in that regard is only a polished version of Tony Lumpkin. You want to go to Mr. Hardcastle's. He tells you you can never get there; he describes it as a "long, dark, boggy, dirty, dangerous way "; dilates on the terrors of Quagmire Marsh, Squash Lane, and Crackskull Common ; and indicates four roads—you must " be sure to take only one of them " —which he knows perfectly well lead nowhere. In manner and motive only he differs from Mr. Lumpkin. He does not want you to get the heiress, and it is with perfect breeding that he takes care that you shan't.

Examine the whole of the noble Marquess's life history; trace him from the Under-Secretary larva of forty-six years ago to the Elder Statesman imago of to-day; follow him through every step of his career—Simla, Ottawa, War Office, Foreign Office, leadership of the House of Lords—and the main impression given is that of superficies claiming the dimensions of a solid. Neither depth nor bulk is there. He has every quality appertaining to the wise man except wisdom itself. His moderation is notable where courage is the only currency; he is bold where Danton would step with fear and trembling; outspoken where secrecy is imperative; secretive where a frank word might work wonders. He does everything the wise statesman might, except at the right time and in the right place.

Generally the charge of inconsistency against a public man is the dullest of cheap sneers. The deadly fact concerning Lord Lansdowne's changes is that they are really consistent; he has an infallible instinct, not for the lost cause, but for the cause that ought to be lost.

He was a Whig when Whiggism was the least liberal of political faiths; he became a Conservative in its late bad manner; he pursued an adventurous foreign policy as Foreign Minister, and now argues in retirement for a stultifying peace; he claimed for the House of Lords powers that upset the balance of the Constitution, and then admitted by his reform proposals that peers were wholly unfit to exercise even their admitted functions; in the present war his influence, above that of any subject born this side of St. George's Channel, has made Ireland a material and moral liability to the Alliance. As a Parliamentary strategist he resembles that Duke of York who marched his men up a very high hill and marched them down again. For both operations no doubt textbook authority may be found. But generalship does not consist alone in doing right things. They must be done at the right time. Lord Lansdowne is the kind of man who would treat as dangerous a cow that is only aching to be milked, and, having vexed it to madness, would seek to placate it by the offer of a nice crimson overcoat. He is gruff to the lamb and the coney; he is mild courtesy to the tiger.

Since the famous letter of last autumn a singular company has gathered round the ambiguous standard of the Marquess. These men may quite misunderstand his purpose, but they are themselves well understood, and, since the Marquess has never disowned them, it is not unfair to suppose him willing to use them. Socialists, Syndicalists, Quakers, representatives of cosmopolitan finance, aristocratic Liberal intellectuals—a more ill-assorted group was never brought together by flood or prairie fire. To most of them Lord Lansdowne two years ago was an English Junker; now one reads of such a marvel as a "Lansdowne Labour Committee." Yet Lord Lansdowne was probably never farther than he is to-day from the moral position of the Outhwaites, Lee Smiths, Ramsay MacDonalds, and Noel Buxtons. The worst that can be said of these is that they fight in unprincipled fashion for a principle. For what principles does the Marquess of Lansdowne stand?

He has no Quakerish scruples against war, or he would not have supported Mr. Chamberlain in his belief that the conquest of the Boer Republics would be cheap, short, and profitable. He has no passion against secret diplomacy; he hurried the Anglo-Japanese treaty through hugger-mugger, without reflection as to its ultimate consequences, because the need of the moment appeared to be the checkmating of Russia. He made tentative advances towards a German alliance before he set about laying the foundations of the Entente Cordiale, and in both cases hour-to-hour expediency was the only motive. He coolly tore open the sores of Ireland

merely to complicate the issue his timorous violence
had raised in English politics. Then he tried to throw
into the quarrel the Colonies, and finally the Army.
Truly there is little in this record to suggest that at
seventy-three his heart beats in tumultuous sympathy
with Mr. Snowden, or that his tired eyes have glorious
visions of universal brotherhood.

A more congruous explanation may be suggested
of the attitude which has brought Lord Lansdowne
all this strange homage. Lord Lansdowne is an aristocrat of a quite peculiar class. I believe he has in
him a few drops of the blood of Talleyrand, and something of that great sceptic's temperament has also
come down to him. When all Paris was repeating
that in a fortnight the Emperor would have crossed
the Niemen, Talleyrand's only comment was " Mais
à quoi bon passer le Niemen ?" Talleyrand happened
to be right in this instance. But " A quoi bon ?" is
the natural comment of the unmilitary aristocrat,
who has little emotion and much interest, who is too
big to take the vulgar view of martial glories, and
possibly too little for the only passions that make
war respectable. War, yes, for things that seem
worth the price. Have there not always been wars
of that common-sense kind? But war that is piling
up debt at the rate of seven millions a day, that
means working-class unrest, super-taxes, land taxes,
taxes of all kinds to be paid, not merely by the
creatures who die to-morrow, but by the families that
decay for ever—à quoi bon?

After all, the whole thing may well seem a sordid
stupidity to this cool grandee. He belongs to the
Victorian time, when our sleeping partnership with
Prussia enabled us to go lightly armed and lightly
taxed. It was an ideal arrangement—our Navy
keeping the seas, the German Empire keeping the
Continent, each agreeing that there could be no real
quarrel between the whale and the elephant. Pan-

German stupidity, which must have all, upset this admirable theory. Even our Eldest Statesmen had to take warning by the portents of the last fifteen years. But that is not to say that they have ceased to regret the old days, or that they would not welcome them back if it were feasible. And what if we have really backed the wrong horse?

In this mood it is natural to take stock of the situation. Alsace-Lorraine? The Trentino? Poland? " Self-determination " for the serfs of the House of Habsburg? We can imagine the courtly shrug of the shoulder Lord Lansdowne must give when he revises these idealist war aims. Why should he pant for the resurrection of Poland when he has so long politely denied any imperfections in the government of Ireland?

The League of Nations? Yes. But is it the League of Nations according to President Wilson that he favours? Is it not rather a League of Nations such as Count Hertling had in mind? Mr. Wilson sees in his policy the only means by which the common sense and instinctive morality of the common man shall triumph over the follies of the wise and the sordid ambitions of the great. Lord Lansdowne appears to contemplate some new Holy Alliance that will guarantee permanence to another artificial re-casting of the map of Europe. It is not surprising that long ago he discerned in German statesmanship a returning reasonableness not generally apparent. Perhaps he and Count Hertling were not so far apart. The Englishman has better manners and better morals than the Bavarian, but each may view mankind from much the same standpoint. For each the thing that has been is the thing that must be; there can be nothing new under the sun. Louvain will go the way of Magdeburg; the *Lusitania* will be forgotten. The new democratic heaven of the Washington professor shall pass away; the old hell of aristocratic, plutocratic, or autocratic Europe shall not pass away. Let us forget the things of time, and occupy ourselves with the eternal. The fickle mob will forget, and we, the Olympian gods, will have nothing to remember except such taxation as we cannot decently pass on. Our wives, our daughters, have nothing to complain of; our sons may have fallen, but our houses remain.

So, no doubt, argued the seeming wise Britons who made treaties with Hengist and Horsa; so argued the seeming wise Saxons who agreed to pay Danegelt; so argued the seeming wise Roman patricians who bought off the Vandals and Huns. Their letters are not preserved, but they were probably filled with acute observations on the essential moderation of an enemy still burning and slaying and treaty-breaking. They probably abounded, also, in suggestions of domestic trouble if counsels of reason should be long disregarded, and of the ruin of civilization if peace should be long delayed.

The seeming wise man is generally short-sighted, and Lord Lansdowne is no exception. He seems at bottom to build on a common interest between the classes in this country and the classes in Prussia to resist any movement from below. He forgets, on the one hand, that Prussia has no kind of loyalty, and that even if we earned the wages of infamy she would not pay them; we cannot get back to the old relations by mere surrender and betrayal. He forgets, on the other hand, that the only dangerous England is a half-defeated England. If the cause triumphs, our oligarchs may survive; at worst they will be not unkindly shelved: If not—— But I make no pretence to second sight.

VISCOUNT NORTHCLIFFE

FOUR years ago Viscount Northcliffe was merely a newspaper miracle. Lately many people have speculated, not unsympathetically, whether the country would accept him as Prime Minister, with the powers of a dictator, for it is understood that he would take office on no other terms. Many others regard his present indirect power as one of the chief dangers of the State. Outside the circle of his business activities Lord Northcliffe used to be regarded as a kind of joke. Now friends and foes—and he has both in plenty—agree in taking him most seriously.

It was said of Napoleon III. that he deceived all Europe twice : first when he pretended to be a fool, and secondly when he pretended to be a statesman. Possibly there has been a somewhat similar misjudgment regarding Lord Northcliffe. He was certainly underrated in his vigorous youth; it may be that in middle age the blaze of his prestige is too blinding for a reasonable estimate of his real qualities. Apart from the artist sort, he is, of all the men I ever met, he who best satisfies my conception of genius. I hasten to add that I reject altogether the definition of genius as the capacity for taking infinite pains, and equally Carlyle's idea of it as a general power of intelligence capable alike of writing Shakespeare's sonnets or ruling a State. Lord Northcliffe's genius is like that of certain men for games of skill : it can coexist with something very like general mediocrity. Lord Northcliffe's genius is perhaps as narrow as that of a great chess-player. But nobody who has had the privilege of observing his methods as a newspaper man—he is very much more than a newspaper proprietor—can possibly fail to acknowledge a power quite different in kind as well as in degree from mere business or professional acumen.

Lord Northcliffe, in his proper business, has the gift of intuitive perception in extraordinary measure. He possesses a supreme instinct for the right thing in the sense of the expedient thing. He knows exactly what the public wants, or rather what the public would want if it knew how to make its wants known. A good many caterers in his line are shrewd enough judges of what the common man says and feels to-day. It is Lord Northcliffe's special gift that he knows what the common man will be saying the day after to-morrow, and says it in advance. In great things and small, he has always been a little ahead of his rivals. He was in the forefront of the cycle boom, both as a writer and a racer. He was the first to vitalize the old scrap journalism of the *Tit-Bits* type, to infuse into its Victorian formlessness and respectability new elements appealing less to the middle class than to the first flower of Board School culture. He aimed at the "man in the street," and hit him hard in every issue of *Answers*, with its "strong sex interest," its "Five Pounds a Week for Life" competitions, its attention to the "romance" of crime, food, and money, and its general air of knowingness.

Answers was Alfred Harmsworth's campaign of Italy. As its conductor he reached the high-water mark of his genius. Great men in the making are always more wonderful than great men made. After the 18th Brumaire all was comparatively simple for Napoleon; the real miracle was his early career. After *Answers* Alfred Harmsworth could only repeat himself with variations. He bought the moribund *Evening News*, "Answerized" it, and made it pay. He brought out the *Daily Mail* as a morning *Answers*, with the best cable service money could buy. He made one mistake in his penny *Daily Mirror* for moneyed women; the moneyed women would not pay the penny. But that failure he almost instantaneously turned into a gigantic success by appealing to millions who had never taken a newspaper before. Within a week of the change from good fashion blocks to poor pictures every office boy and milliner's apprentice was buying "the world's only halfpenny picture paper." Lord Northcliffe, with an eye like Napoleon's for the "enemy masses," had suddenly guessed that brains are to eyes as units to tens, and that the mind too inert to read even a serious paragraph may find pleasure in a news picture and information in its "caption."

There is some significance in Lord Northcliffe's choice of heroes—Dickens in letters, Napoleon in history. Dickens he admires for the sureness with which he aimed at the heart of the masses, Napoleon for the way in which he controlled men and got things done. The truth is that he is himself a sort of composite parody of the two men. His message to the common man is perhaps not worth delivering, but he gets it delivered. The things he has got done may not have been worth doing, but he has no living equal in the art of getting those things done.

And he has also the Napoleonic gift of enslaving the intellects of other men without recourse to vulgar tyranny. The Jesuit had to be like a corpse in the hands of his superior. In the Carmelite order of journalism the neophyte must yield a similar obedience. He must give, not only his work, but his spirit. He may gain little or much by the bargain. He may rise to twenty thousand a year, with a knighthood, many motor-cars, and appurtenances to match. Or he may remain a mere cog in that great machine. But on every fragment of human metal in the fabric, whether common cast-iron or finely lacquered brass, is stamped the motto and device of the master. Gurth with his brass collar was less the born thrall

of Cedric than the Carmelite editor of Lord Northcliffe. For Gurth could at least think his own
thoughts, and the editor's thoughts are prescribed
for him.

It has been said of Lord Northcliffe that he was the
first man to build a factory in Bohemia. He has certainly gone far towards industrializing journalism,
and in doing so has given it a commercial stability
and an intellectual flightiness oddly in contrast. The
shares of his concerns have more than the stolidity of
Government securities; it is their editorial opinions
that fluctuate madly. This levity is partially due,
no doubt, to the constitutional jerkiness of Lord
Northcliffe's intelligence. He thinks in headlines and
works in "stunts." He has been steady in but one
thing, the consolidation of his business; and that
business has been largely built up on the flexibility of
his mind on public questions. But there is possibly
another reason for the eccentricity of his course. I
said that he greatly admires Napoleon and Dickens.
Napoleon shut up the deputies; Dickens retained
through life a massive contempt for the House of
Commons. From his earliest days Alfred Harmsworth seems to have been equally attracted and
irritated by politics. He desired the double pleasure
of despising the game and playing a part in it.
Though he might speak of the House of Commons as
an antiquated vestry, he tried to enter it through the
borough of Portsmouth. Portsmouth would have
none of him, and from the day of that defeat he has
consistently belittled representative institutions, and
assailed politicians of all parties with a contempt
sometimes just, but seldom entertained on just
grounds. His only consistency has been the consistency of hatred for a theatre for which he has not
the industry, or perhaps the talent, to qualify.

To some who knew him best, it was rather surprising that he should have accepted, first, a baronetcy,

and then a peerage, from Mr. Balfour. In the first place he somewhat diminished the independence which he had by this time, after some attempt to play the party game, adopted as his line; in the second, he parted with a considerable source of moral strength. For in his young days he did stand for a kind of democratic reality. He has never had much eye for the greatest—it is remarkable, for example, that he has never brought out a really first-class writer in any line—but at one period no man had a surer perception of the mere fool, however gilded. Holding himself aloof from society, refusing to be entangled in any set, busying himself solely in his wealth and newspaper influence, he might in a negative way have been of considerable service to the country in his part of independent critic. But since his ennoblement a certain degeneration has been noticeable. His campaigns have tended to become personal vendettas. He is no longer outside party; his judgments and quarrels are party judgments and quarrels, though his party consists only of one. It is never quite certain whether any step he takes is dictated by principle; there is always the possibility that he has made a new friend or quarrelled with an old one.

This suspicion, far more than any single mistake or failure during the war, is responsible for the widespread resentment of his Press methods. He has generally contrived to put himself wrongly on the right side. His purely official work is said to have been fairly successful, but certainly of no such inspired character as to justify the arrogance with which he declines to join a Government without ruling it. On that question of his being accepted as a sort of dictator, little need be said. The cook who cannot produce a dinner of some sort without complete reconstruction of the kitchen is not the cook one would naturally put in charge of a kitchen when reconstructed. One distrusts entirely the "strong" man who can only work in conditions he himself prescribes. We have to take the world and the British Constitution as we find them; both are profoundly unsatisfactory, but not to be changed in a hurry.

Lord Northcliffe has one of the "strong" man's weaknesses. He has never been crossed, has never had to argue a case, has never had to withstand in his own person a personal attack, since he was a boy. He has pilloried all sorts of people; he has never been pilloried except by rival newspapers, and the public quite rightly refuses to get excited over Pott and Slurk heroics. "Newspaper shrapnel," as he calls it, he can ignore; and he has never let himself come within the range of a really heavy gun. He will not meet an attack in the Lords; he takes part only in that sort of public gathering where the decencies permit of no plain speaking. In his office he is surrounded by stipendiary cherubim and seraphim, raising an eternal chorus of "Brainy, brainy, brainy." For a quarter of a century he has been a Commander of the Faithful, with cunning mixers of sherbet and deft manipulators of the bowstring around him. Hence that curiously arrogant shyness, that eagerness for power without responsibility, that passion for publicity and shrinking from its consequences, that make him at once the most and the least known man in English public life.

Caught young, before the mischievous kittenishness of *Answers* days had hardened into cathood, he might have developed into a considerable statesman, though it may be questioned whether that real but narrow genius of his, so suited to its tiny purpose, could have been expanded to embrace the larger things of life. Even now he might, under due control, do useful work in some department in which he is really interested—matters aerial, for example. But Pegasus will not work in harness, and it would be madness to give him the reins.

MR. AUSTEN CHAMBERLAIN

MR. AUSTEN CHAMBERLAIN'S return to office was welcomed mainly on the ground that he is an honest man, and condemned mainly on the ground that he is a politician.

Regarding the first point, the implication is sufficiently alarming. Lord Morley, in his last book, tells how, as Irish Secretary, he " turned down " a nomination to the County Bench because the person in question had the character of being "moderately honest." His lordship took the old-fashioned view that moderate honesty is as unsatisfactory as reasonable chastity. We have been accustomed to look on integrity in public life not as a virtue in itself, but as the indispensable foundation of all other virtues. One can imagine Gladstone's feelings had he been publicly described as a statesman of conspicuous honesty and some capacity. Have we really arrived at the pass when we must be told that if the country is not safe in a statesman's hands, at least the country's safe is safe?

For the moment we will assume, however rashly, that every public man is honest, and pass from Mr. Chamberlain's chiefly advertised virtue to his chiefly advertised crime. It is, perhaps, useless to try to stem the cataract of nonsense now roaring against "professional politicians." But it may be said at once that Mr. Chamberlain's solitary claim to a place in the Government resides in this very fact that he is first and foremost a politician—that is, that he has a considerable grip of Parliamentary things and much knowledge of official ways. True, he is not the sort of man one would naturally choose to ride the whirl-wind and direct the storm. " Pitt is to Addington as London is to Paddington," wrote Canning to another amiable mediocrity. Mr. Chamberlain is decidedly Paddingtonian. His abilities, though sedulously cultivated, are at best second-rate; he lacks, above all, power; he rather reminds one of those pallid city youths who, with a bedroom exerciser, attain a certain muscular development, but never achieve " punch " or natural vigour.

In the case of such a person it is merely foolish to blame Mr. Muldow's system for his rather unsatisfactory condition; the question is rather what he would have been without Mr. Muldow. When one hears an Oxford graduate talking great nonsense (which happens occasionally) the first tendency may be to condemn the University; second and sounder thoughts prompt the inquiry what sort of nonsense the same man would have talked had he stopped short at a primary school. Certainly it is an unprofitable business sending poor grist to a first-class mill, and the care lavished on Mr. Chamberlain's political education doubtless might have been better expended on another subject. But to suggest that Government, of all trades, is one in which talents are not improved by training is merely silly, and to complain that Mr. Chamberlain knows at least part of his trade is surely irrational.

One part of his trade he knows very well indeed. He is an excellent House of Commons man. He would probably make a very fair Leader of the House, and it would not be surprising to learn that the astute Prime Minister, with an eye to possibilities, had earmarked him for that position should it fall vacant. Second-rate men often make first-rate leaders, just as some extremely brilliant statesmen have failed calamitously in that capacity. The House of Commons is like a certain type of horse, which will allow a favourite child to manage it, and will respond to a master whip, but shows every vice in the hands of a semi-competent. Some men dominate the House by sheer force of character; others conquer by tact; still others get their way because the House likes them, and knows they like the House. The latter was the secret of the conspicuous success of very ordinary people like W. H. Smith and "C.-B.," and Mr. Chamberlain might well develop in the same direction. He has, it is true, some handicaps from which they were free. In humour he is slenderly endowed, and he has not that cheerful sense of his own limitations which is often the greatest asset of the second-rate statesman, enabling him, without raising jealousies, to guide men with whom he could not seriously compete.

"C.-B.," by shrewd judgment and good-humour, succeeded in managing a team of which seven individuals out of ten were his intellectual superiors. Mr. Chamberlain has not quite learned that *savoir faire* which is based ultimately on perfect self-knowledge. There are times when he still gives the impression of believing himself to be a statesman in the grand manner. But the amiable illusion has shown signs of weakening since the Tariff Reform days; it suffered one great shock when Mr. Bonar Law was chosen Unionist leader, and another when the Mesopotamia report was issued. In regard to that melancholy business Mr. Chamberlain's prompt recognition of his responsibility was to his credit, but common sense rebels at fellow-politicians' description of his resignation as a mere quixotry on the part of a man only nominally to blame. Mr. Chamberlain's fault was negative but real. It was not so much that he was wrong as that he was not vigorously enough in the right.

But vigour is just the quality Mr. Chamberlain lacks, though he tries hard to imitate the masterfulness of his father. I once had the singular experience of visiting the house of a rich man with a gruesome hobby. He had spent his life going round the great picture galleries of the world and employing copyists to reproduce their chief treasures. These he put in gorgeous imitations of old Florentine frames, and, at a cost adequate to papering his walls with minor masterpieces, was able to flatter himself that he was surrounded by the highest in art. I am reminded of that disconsolate collection of sham Titians, Rembrandts, and Raphaels, stiff and smooth as anything at Madame Tussaud's, whenever I happen to be at the House of Commons when Mr. Chamberlain is "up." He is so like, yet so unlike, his father. The outlines are there, as in Signor Spaghetti's copies, but there is no vigour of colour, no force of expression, no power of modelling. All is flat and tame. Joseph Chamberlain's words cut like a whip; his anger had sometimes almost the effect of physical shock; his monocle could be as terrifying as the eye of Polyphemus. Mr. Austen's is no more formidable than Mr. Weedon Grossmith's. The elder man penetrated his utterances with real passion. The younger tries to do the same, but his artificial indignation rather recalls the dog that went mad " to serve some private ends." Men easily recover from that sort of bite.

In middle age, Mr. Austen Chamberlain has to some extent dropped conscious imitation, and he is getting to be as much himself as he will ever be. Temperamentally he differs from his father, and is really what his father never was—a Conservative. But he has not shaken off what his father also never lost—that kind of provincialism which one may call suburbanity. With all his great qualities, Joseph Chamberlain retained to the end some trace of Camberwell. He had Mr. Lloyd George's bad habit—the two men have many points of resemblance—of discussing great affairs in a dialect neither stately nor statesmanlike. He was the man of a world rather than a man of the world. He chid foreign Ministers as if they were Irish Members. He told the French to " mend their

manners" with the same readiness that he called
Mr. Dillon a "good judge of traitors." In his
dealings with rural questions he was as Cockney as
Mr. Pickwick at Dingley Dell. With less excuse,
Mr. Austen Chamberlain is even more limited. He
has industriously "got up" the Empire with the
help of the Blue Books, but shows no real understanding of it, and no man in affairs knows less about
Europe. His abilities, such as they are, are simply
suited to the things of the caucus and the House of
Commons. There he makes a quite respectable display. He always speaks neatly, and sometimes, as
when moved over the Press attacks on Sir William
Robertson, with force and point. Add that he is a
fair administrator, and you have said all that can
be said.

That, with so slender an equipment, Mr. Chamberlain can hardly be called a failure is surely sufficient
rebuttal to the unintelligent outcry against the
"professional politician." That poverty of political
talent which has occasioned the demand for "business
men" is, in fact, chiefly due to the increasing domination of the House of Commons by elderly tradesmen.
A seat in Parliament is no longer the object of young
(and poor) ambition; the House of Commons is
rather a Tom Tiddler's ground where the "arrived"
grub for ribands and titles. If any moral is to be
drawn from Mr. Chamberlain's position it is the
need of something to replace the old patronage system
which secured a steady supply of brilliant youngsters
for the public service.

Our "democratic" system has done away with the
one valuable feature of the borough-mongering days
—the search for talent irrespective of wealth and
social position. But it has greatly intensified the
reverence paid to the hereditary principle. The
owner of a dozen rotten boroughs might allot six to
his friends and relations, but he wanted to get political

value out of the rest; hence the hungry quest for brains and the rise of Pitt, Canning, Gladstone, and so many others. If Mr. Chamberlain is found "indispensable" because he has learned the tricks of the trade, and is still not quite a first-rate man, the inference would seem plain. Instead of declaring that there are no tricks to be learned, and laying down the principle that in politics there shall be only amateur players, it would be more intelligent to teach those tricks to young men of real talent. But that would mean in many cases a preference for plain · Smith and Brown over Vavassour-Smith and Ponsonby-Brown, and it may be doubted whether British snobbery, more rampant than ever in the decline of English aristocracy, would assent to so levelling a doctrine.

THE "MORNING POST" AND
MR. H. A. GWYNNE

THERE are one or two instances of men who began life as footmen shaking off all trace of servile origin. Craggs, the peculating Secretary of State of South Sea Bubble times, was, however immoral, no laughing-stock socially or mentally; and there has been an example in our own time of an ex-servant whom it requires a strong effort to remember in connection with plush and powder.

But in general there hangs round the "gentleman's gentleman" a flavour of ridicule that follows him through life, and the manners and mannerisms of the servants' hall are apt to cling to the most successful of the class. Thus the *Morning Post* has never quite outlived the reputation, or indeed the habits, of its early days. True, it is no longer, as it used to be, the laughter of the wits. In early Victorian days the extraordinary English of its leading articles was as much a joke as its reverential attention to the doings of the great. Thackeray is never tired of jeering at it, though one feels uneasily that he always looked the paper through to see whether his own name was given as attending a "rout" or a dinner party. The Tories, whom it served with valet-like respect, treated it—like a valet. Macaulay in 1831 put on record his view of its importance as a political force. Speaking of a duel that was fought by its editor in 1777, he says: "It certainly seems almost incredible to a person living in our time that any human being should ever have stopped to fight with a writer on the *Morning Post.*"

To-day most of that is changed. The *Morning Post* is the most individual of all the London morning papers. It is also the best written. Its chief contributors really are scholars, though, like ladies, when young and fair, they have the gift to know it, and occasionally annoy by a display of elementary classical lore. It still makes a feature of those fascinating paragraphs regarding increases in aristocratic families, engagements and marriages of "gentlemen of fashion" and "ladies of quality," and the dignified obsequies of all, from a Duke downwards, who can afford its rather high charges for "personal announcements." But, editorially at least, this department no longer dominates. It was otherwise only a few years ago. A distinguished literary man was once invited by the late Lord Glenesk to take the editorial chair. He waited patiently for his lordship to outline the attitude of the paper to certain questions at that moment assuming a new importance. Instead of attending to such minor matters his recently created lordship dwelt on the extreme importance of having names wholly accurate and in their right order. The point was elaborated until the candidate, who joined to a high regard for the nobility and gentry of these

islands some sense of humour and proportion, remarked that what seemed to be really wanted was
a proof-reader, and took his leave.

Such an incident, when taken alone, might give
a poor impression of the mental standing of Algernon
Borthwick. Yet it was he, the highly educated son
of Peter Borthwick—a shrewd self-made Scotsman,
who had acquired the paper during one of its recurring
crises—who laid the foundations of the *Morning Post*
as we now know it. Algernon Borthwick, clever,
pleasant, a great respecter of persons, cautiously
enterprising, extraordinarily limited, but the more
efficient for his purposes through those limitations,
might have proceeded direct from the imagination
of Samuel Warren, the author of that perfect snob-
novel, *Ten Thousand a Year*. Much of his ability,
something of his thrifty disposition, and not a little
of the asperity which tempered his veneration for the
upper classes, have descended to his daughter, who
married in 1893 the seventh Earl Bathurst.

Under her control the *Morning Post* has gradually
abandoned the deferential " as-your-lordship-pleases "
manner of its earlier days. While the old *Times*
adopted of set policy the pose of independence, with
an acknowledged bias in favour of the Government
of the day, while the *Standard* of Mudford days spoke
plain English about its own leaders, the *Morning
Post* was content to " say ditto to Mr. Burke." It
would probably be saying " ditto " still but for the
fact that changes in Fleet Street ended by leaving it
the only true-blue Tory morning paper in London.
The *Standard* declined and died; the *Times* changed
hands and methods; the *Telegraph* did not change,
but remained what it has always been, mainly intent
on its advertising columns. Conscious of its new
position, the *Morning Post* began to indulge an
autocratic temper of which it had not hitherto been
suspected.

Readers of Thackeray will remember that masterly
scene in which Mr. Morgan, who had submissively
combed Major Pendennis's wigs and prepared his
footbath for years, suddenly called on that old war-
rior to stand and deliver. "Shall I wring your old
head off and drownd yer in that pail of water? Do
you think I'm a-going to bear your confounded old
harrogance, you old Wigsby?" And so forth and
so on. Far be it from me to compare this hypo-
critical old blackmailer, grown shamefully rich on
menial service, to the most "high-class" of English
newspapers, which was content to claim not the
largest, but the "best" circulation. But there is
really some suggestion in Mr. Morgan's insurgence
of the change that came over the *Morning Post*
when it was left the solitary oracle of old-fashioned
Toryism. In its old days it had been the well-trained
footman; in its new style it rather suggests a flustered
and revolting butler.

The change has not quite synchronized with the
reign of its present editor, Mr. Howell A. Gwynne.
The revolt against Mr. Balfour, the alliance with
Confederates, Die-Hards, "antique bantams of the
fighting breed" (as the *Morning Post* once lyrically
described the venerable Lord Halsbury), *et hoc genus
omne*, dated rather earlier, and may perhaps be explained, not only by disagreements on policy, but by
some obscure prejudice against the Cecil family. But
certainly the peculiar wildness of the *Morning Post*
has attained its zenith under the editorial direction of
this talented Welshman.

Mr. Gwynne is a fighting rather than a thinking
editor. He knows everybody in politics, but strangely
little of political questions. Though he gives little
evidence of any grave study of economic problems,
he is a Tariff Reformer, as Falstaff was a respecter of
royalty, "on instinct." He is a strong Imperialist,
on instinct again, plus the inspiration of Lord Milner,

his ideal in statesmanship, and Joseph Chamberlain, to whose spell he succumbed when he accompanied that great man to South Africa in his Reuter correspondent days. In literature he has one idol, Mr. Kipling, and several *bêtes noires,* of whom Mr. H. G. Wells may be taken as the type. He hates aliens, Nonconformists, Radicals, Welshmen, Irish Catholics, Humanitarians, Free Traders, and Anti-vivisectionists about equally, and probably thinks they are all very much the same thing. His experience as a war correspondent gave him a real love of arms and armies, and no great abhorrence of war itself. This war he can hardly like; the wars for his money are snug, profitable, picturesque wars, ending in more of the map painted red.

Force is his remedy for everything. He was for force in South Africa. He is for force in Ireland. He has seriously recommended, during times of industrial trouble, systematic siege operations in the affected areas. He laughs to scorn the notion that this war is being waged, or should be waged, for any other than the narrowest national objects. He refuses altogether to believe that the common man, whose blood is being spilt, can have any ideal but his own terribly simple one of a foreigner-tight, all-red, self-supporting, self-sufficing, imperialistic, aggressive, and thoroughly vulgar "Empire." He will laugh at German "Kultur" notions. But he is all for a British "Kultur" as illiberal, less brutal indeed, but perhaps even more sordid, because it would imply a frank contempt for intellect which, to do the German justice, is not his characteristic fault.

These are Mr. Gwynne's quite honest ideals. They would seem to distinguish him in no way from some of the dullest of living Englishmen. But this intellectual simplicity is combined with a capacity for manœuvre that will secure his name some prominence when the secret history of the last fifteen years is

laid open. He has a talent for influencing men much
more able than himself. He was a very considerable
force in the Budget fight. He did much to precipitate
the Parliament Act crisis. He had a great deal to
do with the deposition of Mr. Balfour and the sealing
of the fatal Unionist-Carsonite alliance. He worked
as hard to get Mr. Lloyd George into power as he has
latterly worked to get him out. With prejudices firmly
fixed, and all else in a state of flux, it is not surprising
that there is a sort of stormy unity in his journalistic
career; few men have been more violently and variously
wrong.

With more balance, and equal distinction in
writing, the *Morning Post* might under him be a
tremendous power for evil; without the piquant
charm of his chief leader-writer's style, it would be
merely contemptible. Things being as they are, it
is a sort of Puck-Mephistopheles, chiefly effective in
its more freakish side. Its graver plots have a habit
of miscarrying. But it can always snatch three-legged
stools from beneath the unsuspecting, and create a
general atmosphere of commotion.

The *Morning Post* once boldly likened itself to a
toad. That is the last comparison on which the polite
critic would venture. But since it has been made, it
may be adopted in order to conclude on a note of just
compliment. "The toad, ugly and venomous, wears
yet a precious jewel in its head." The venom of the
Morning Post is all too apparent. Its valuable
qualities are less obviously displayed. They include
an absence of vulgarity on all non-political topics, an
abhorrence of sensational methods, a generally enlightened literary judgment, honesty and balance in
the presentment of news, a consistent hostility to the
more sordid forms of "influence" and political intrigue, and a "City page" of outstanding ability.
The pity is that the *corpus sanum* does not lodge a
spirit quite in keeping.

MR. WALTER LONG

MR. LONG is a time-defying type. Of course, the years have had their usual physical effect on him. They have somewhat enlarged the tonsure of a constitutional baldness. They have deepened the russet of his cheeks, slightly blanched his blonde moustache, taken something from the once ramrod-erectness of his horseback seat. But mentally it is the same Long : as he was in the beginning, he is now, and shall be.

In Mr. Long the type overpowers the individual. True, he has a personality. But so has a pedigree bull. It may be roguish or gentle, brindled or red, or black and white, with its own tastes and prejudices in the matter of hay and mangels. But, after all, the main fact about it is that it is a Shorthorn or a Hereford. When you have stated the breed you have said all that is necessary in a general way.

Mr. Long is a pedigree squire. Few others are so genuine. The Longs have neither ascended into the ranks of the great nor sunk into the general mass. They have lacked the ambition and ability of certain other ancient families, and, on the other hand, they have never been given to the vices which dissipate patrimonies. For centuries pursuing the safe path of mediocrity, they have kept their own, and grown with the times. There were West-Country Longs, doubtless, before there was a county of Wilts ; it is certain that Wilts had Longs before England had a Parliament, and almost since Parliament was Wilts has sent Longs to it. One Long sat during the Wars of the Roses. Another figured in one of the stormy Parliaments of Charles I. A third held office of some dignity under the Merry Monarch, and if one cared to rummage in Dryasdust one would be pretty certain to find in every reign a Long who was something.

but not very much. No Long ever sounded all the depths and shoals of honour, or played the part of the little wanton boys who swim on bladders. The family produced no subtle thinker or ambitious plotter. One never reads of a Long exchanging conceits with Sir Thomas More, or verses with Spenser, or maxims with Bacon, or guilty confidences with Shaftesbury. If any Long swam in a gondola we may be sure he never came back that " Diavolo Incarnato," the Italianate Englishman. If any Long shared Charles I.'s travels we may be sure he carried everywhere with him the air and the accent of the chalk downs.

Mr. Walter Long, like his ancestors, is unadulterated squire, with a great deal of the good and some of the not so good that belongs to that character. But he has one gift that distinguishes him from the generality of the genus. He is a talking squire. He has the talent of articulate speech. He can talk on any subject. He does not talk well; but a talking squire is like a talking horse; as Johnson says, " the wonder, sir, is not that the thing is not done well, but that it is done at all." I remember Mr. Long when he first entered Parliament for the Northern Division of Wiltshire in the pre-Distribution Act days. He was then very young; in fact, he made the neat and original point of apologizing for a fault that time would cure. But he spoke without hesitation or remorse, and he has been speaking unhesitatingly and remorselessly ever since.

Of course, this fluency would not of itself have advanced Mr. Long to the Front Bench. Had he come from the suburbs of a North-Country town the healthy pink of his complexion would have remained an ornament of the unofficial benches. But he enjoyed, like Lord Chaplin, the advantage of being the representative of an important class in which the capacity of coherent expression is rare. Lord Chaplin,

who possesses the same easy power of aqueous eloquence, together with an elephantine majesty peculiarly his own, would probably have gone farther than
Mr. Long had he not been carried away by his Pro-
tectionist leanings at a time when Fair Trade was
banned as a dead and damned heresy by the Tory
Caucus. Mr. Long made no such mistake. At
farmers' ordinaries and puppy-walking luncheons in
Wilts and Gloucestershire he might drop hints that
made the beer mugs or champagne glasses rattle with
a joyous music, but in Whitehall he was strictly
orthodox—until the time came when it was orthodox
to profess Protection once more.

In this timely conformity and equally timely conversion we have the man. For Mr. Long's eyes, so
frank, so honest, so English in their attractive colour-
scheme of torquoise in a coral setting, have always
been fixed on the main chance politically, and have
not disdained to regard the main chance in private
matters either. He is a shrewd man in a land deal,
and he has a good deal of land, both in England
and Ireland, where he benefited largely by the will of
his grandfather, Mr. William Hume-Dick, from whom
he derives his second name. He holds the simple
faith of the squire, that a man has a right to do
what he likes with his own, and that land exists
chiefly for the nurture of landlords. The English
squire is, perhaps, the most manly, honourable,
healthy-minded, and selfish man this earth has produced—too fond of sucking blood to shed it uselessly,
too lazy and too careful of his own mental comfort
to tyrannize in the fashion of a Prussian Junker, too
proud to go back on his word except to inferiors,
too fond of sport and jollity to live ungenially among
his own people. But his compromises have been as
fatal as other despots' logical cruelties, and under his
open smile the English countryside has become largely
an open and smiling desert. We do well to make the

most of men like Mr. Long, to applaud them as the fine flower of our manhood. For truly we have reared them at a prodigious cost.

It is not a little singular that, while at Westminster people think little of Mr. Long as a statesman and much of him as a county magnate, in Wiltshire he is regarded as an inspired politician but as nothing very special as a landowner or a sportsman. Rood Ashton, with all its dead and gone Longs, is a small affair beside Badminton or Longleat. Mr. Long, who hunts occasionally, is a minor hero compared with those who "show sport" six days in the week. It is just this action and reaction of Westminster on Wiltshire and Wiltshire on Westminster that have been the secret of Mr. Long's solid success in politics. Wiltshire said, "Send Mr. Long to the talking-shop; he knows how to talk." Westminster said "Long is not brilliant, certainly, but he knows all about fertilizers, turnips, foot-and-mouth disease, gooseberry mildew, and how to talk to Hodge; he's safe, he isn't faddy, and one must have one man who can be put up to reply without a stutter to Radical land nonsense." Once in the Cabinet, Mr. Long showed, as in the case of the Local Government Act of 1888, a certain Quarter Sessions shrewdness and Board of Guardians common sense that marked him as a useful man in his way, and the tradition of his indispensability in a Conservative Government rapidly took root.

If we may believe a once well-known story, the inclusion at last became automatic. "Who's that very pleasant-looking man?" Lord Salisbury is said to have asked of Mr. Balfour, as Mr. Long bowed to them in Downing Street. "That," explained Mr. Balfour, "is the President of the Local Government Board, Walter Long." "Ah," said the Prime Minister, "I felt sure I had seen that face somewhere." One wonders what the ironic Cecil, a great man in his kind, would have thought had he foreseen that in a very few years the party he led, rich in general talent and graced by one or two fine intellects, would be divided on the question whether the pleasant-looking squire, or Mr. Chamberlain's rather disappointing son, or a Glasgow iron merchant still unknown, should command it.

The choice of Mr. Long might have been happier than that of Mr. Bonar Law, for at least he does stand for something quite definite. He is a plain Tory of the Shires, and not a fantastic Conservative of the suburbs. He is "out" simply for himself and his friends, for land, Church, and the trade. I believe he has, or had, relatives in each. Under him Toryism might have gone back to its old simplicity for awhile, healthily slumbering until a more vital spirit arose. But such speculations are idle. The practical point is that Mr. Long, having once been, to adapt the Papal formula, "Prime Ministerable," was confirmed for life in his right to be considered in the party, and so, when the first War Coalition was formed, the claims of Mr. Long, in the classic phrase, "could not be ignored." The Coalition Cabinet must be "representative"; who so representative as the squire of Rood Ashton? Unfortunately, Mr. Long has been far too representative to be used to the best purpose.

He has qualities, to be quite fair, which might have fitted him for certain Departmental and House of Commons work. He has piloted necessary Bills through Parliament with some skill, and no doubt has worked honestly and well, according to his lights, in Whitehall. But unhappily, so "representative" a man could not be treated merely as a junior Minister. He had to be called into counsel on some of the most important questions before the Cabinet, and Mr. Long is a calamitous counsellor on anything more complex than a dog-muzzling order. It was, for example, a tragic absurdity to call on him to take a principal part in the attempt to straighten out the Irish tangle. His very experience as Irish Secretary was a handicap. For he is rather a vain man, and the fact that he went through a quiet period without grave trouble has given him exaggerated notions of his own capacity as an Irish administrator, and a quite inadequate conception of the situation produced by the crimes and errors of recent years.

It is a sad fact, but the war has rendered Mr. Long obsolete as more than an underling, and he can scarcely be that with his record. There might have been a place for him in the England of ten years ago. To-day he is a political megatherium. For the England of the Longs has passed away. The landed gentry of the cosy Victorian time, with many privileges and no duties save what they found fun or profit in undertaking, can hardly survive in any case. If they survive it will only be by transforming themselves into something unrecognizable. They can no longer maintain themselves on the basis of " showing good sport " and distributing, in virtue of being rich men, poor justice. And even if the class changes by some miracle, Mr. Long at least is unchangeable. The farewell to him will be kindly in form, but definite in effect.

LORD BEAVERBROOK

" As to leaders in parties, nothing is more common than to see them blindly led. The world is governed by go-betweens. These go-betweens influence the persons with whom they carry on the intercourse, by stating their own sense to each of them as the sense of the other ; and thus they reciprocally master both sides."
—BURKE : *Appeal from the New to the Old Whigs.*

IT is nearly thirty-nine years ago since the family circle of the late Rev. William Aitken, Scottish minister, of New Brunswick, Canada, was gladdened by the arrival of a boy baby, who, when he renounced the powers of evil, was given the names of William

and Maxwell. In later life he dropped the first
Christian name and shortened the second, and it was
as Max Aitken, *tout court*, that he became, as early
as twenty-five years of age, a rich man.

It would be interesting to trace the origins of that
fortune which has enabled the Presbyterian clergy-
man's son to play a considerable part in English
affairs, and to become successively Knight, Baronet,
Peer of the Realm, and Minister. Unfortunately a
certain obscurity invests the earlier business life of
Lord Beaverbrook. It is understood that he had a
short and highly successful career in the West Indies
before he set up in business in Halifax and Montreal.
In Canada he achieved great things as a financier and
"bond merchant," and it is certain that, in whatever
pursuits he made money, he made it very rapidly.

In the year 1910, Max Aitken invaded England.
No other verb quite expresses the fact. He came, he
saw, he overcame. In the early months of that year
the mention of his name, in any but a very limited
circle, would have conveyed nothing. At the end of
the year he was well known in the City and even better
known at Westminster. His social and political progress rather recalled that of Mr. Veneering in *Our
Mutual Friend*. People who had known him a fortnight somehow felt they were the chosen comrades of
his boyhood. He rapidly collected round him more
old and intimate friends than the ordinary man makes
in a lifetime. In company with some of these (of at
least three weeks' standing) he went down to Ashton-
under-Lyne, as Mr. Veneering did to Pocket Breeches,
and won a whirlwind election campaign. There was
no resisting his big car, his bevy of tame editors, his
powerful gift of speech.

The next year he was knighted. Mr. Asquith, of
course, was not so conscious of the merits of a political
opponent as to confer this honour of his own initiative.
But it is the custom from time to time to confer a

certain number of honours on the suggestion of the Opposition leader, and Mr. Aitken had by this time won a position in the Unionist Party sufficient to justify Mr. Balfour in putting forward his name. It is safe to say that Mr. Balfour himself had only a formal share in the transaction. His star was already fast declining, and Mr. Aitken was the last man in the world to take an interest in "back numbers." He had allied himself with the extreme Tariff Reformers; he was searching London for a daily paper to push himself and his creed; he was hand-in-glove with those who had already resolved on Mr. Balfour's deposition. The true credit for the bestowal of this honour no doubt belongs to Mr. Bonar Law. He and Mr. Aitken were on close terms of intimacy; they came from the same province; they shared the same economic convictions. It was only natural that Mr. Law should put in a word for his pushful and ambitious friend.

Sir Max, as we must now call him, grew rapidly in political stature. He was one of those members who are seldom heard in the House, but are constantly felt in the Lobbies. Even before he obtained control of a newspaper he exercised considerable influence through journalistic friends, who shared his week-ends and his lightning trips between this country and Canada. Quite impervious to a rebuff, possessing a remarkable talent for finding the weak side of every man, amazingly frank in manner, and extremely subtle in method, he hustled his way into the inner circle of the "Die-Hards." His part in the plot that dethroned Mr. Balfour was undoubtedly considerable, and later he threw the whole weight of his influence on the side of the Ulster extremists. In due course his ambitions for direct newspaper influence were gratified, and in three or four years the mysterious visitor from Canada had attained a power none the less formidable because it was largely exercised from behind cover.

Without a knowledge of these facts it is not easy to

understand the strong feeling created by Lord Beaver-brook's appointment as Director of Propaganda. They are necessary, also, in order to appreciate the part he played in the drama which led to a change of Government in 1916. The full facts are not known. But it is certain that in the movement culminating in Mr. Asquith's retirement the Canadian knight was an actor of prime importance. He was the go-between who, as Burke puts it, often governs by suggestion, and becomes the master of those he seems to serve.

Towards the end of 1916 there was much disunion in the Cabinet and great discontent in the country. Mr. Lloyd George, while on terms of personal friendliness with Mr. Asquith, was profoundly out of sympathy with some features of his policy. He had drawn apart from most of his colleagues, and was in close relations with Sir Edward Carson, who had angrily flung out of the Cabinet a year before in protest against the supposed supineness of the Prime Minister. Mr. Bonar Law was extremely uncomfortable. The debate on the sale of enemy properties in Nigeria, in which he had been placed in a position of antagonism to the extreme Tariff Reformers, had greatly disturbed him, in view of his pledge not to hold office in the Coalition longer than he retained the confidence of his party. Between him and Mr. Lloyd George there was at this time less cordiality than before or after, and events had somewhat strained his relations with Sir Edward Carson. Sir Max Aitken —I am adopting the version given by "An Independent Liberal" in his illuminating little book— used his influence to bring these three together. The history of the crisis is really the history of the scores of meals, breakfasts, dinners, and suppers which these four enjoyed under the friendly roof of the member for Ashton-under-Lyne during the November of 1916.

It is unnecessary here to recall all the attempts at accommodation and the events which led to the final

breach.   Mr. Law was undoubtedly actuated by two
motives, and two only—to improve the administration
and to unify his own party.   Mr. Lloyd George was
unwilling to force Mr. Asquith into resignation,
though determined to get his point.   Sir Edward
Carson was probably well enough pleased with the
actual issue.   That issue was perhaps inevitable.   But
in the sudden frustration of all attempts at compromise we seem to trace the influence of a master of
intrigue.   Somebody gave information on which *The
Times* based its article of December 4, representing
the Prime Minister as having agreed practically to
become a *roi fainéant*, " an irresponsible spectator,"
to borrow Mr. Asquith's own phrase.   That there was
a leakage is certain ; who supplied the facts on which
this insulting gloss was made has never been revealed,
and probably never will be.

Sir Max Aitken survived only a few days the fall of
the Asquith Ministry.   He disappeared for ever, and
Baron Beaverbrook took his place.   In this country
there was little comment at the time on this curious
coincidence.   After all, we are accustomed to the
ennoblement of rich men with no very obvious public
claims.   In the Dominions, on the other hand, titles
are not popular at the best, and the bestowal of this
particular title caused a feeling little understood on
our side of the Atlantic. In honouring Sir Max Aitken
it would really seem that the Prime Minister had not
succeeded in persuading Canada that Canada was
honoured.   Comments described in the House of
Commons as " amazingly frank and even libellous "
appeared in the free-spoken journals of that free land ;
they were read on this side ; and the criticism of Lord
Beaverbrook's appointment as Chief Propagandist was
largely based on these strictures.

On other grounds the attacks made on Lord Beaverbrook's conduct of the Ministry of Information have
so far failed to convince.   True, he is in many respects

quite unfitted for the task. He brings to it neither the appropriate education nor the necessary knowledge of European affairs. The smallest part of that business is drum-beating, cinema-filming, and vulgar advertisement. It demands a deep knowledge of affairs, close touch with European history during the last fifty years, some perception of what part religion still plays in the lives of men, and a delicate sense of what may be called the personality of nations. The coarsest mistakes are possible to a person of small culture, and the hustle and bustle of the shrewd, sharp business man constitute an actual disqualification. But when that is said, there appears no special reason to believe that Lord Beaverbrook is less suitable than any other of the pushful type. He is undoubtedly shrewd, and has done some things which deserve recognition. For example, he has appreciably relaxed the foolish policy of reticence. He has seen the advantage of bringing to the notice of Colonial journalists the real facts of the war. He has done something to break down the wall of misunderstanding between Great Britain and her Allies as to our share in the general burden and sacrifice. Critics, indeed, have been driven to dwell less on what he has done than what he might do.

And that really is the chief strength of their case. Lord Beaverbrook may be, and probably is, a fit recipient of the favour of the Crown, and might, in many capacities, be a highly useful public servant. But there was a crudity about the conferment of his titles that struck many, and it is undeniably a little disquieting to observe the ease with which an ambitious man, coming as a stranger to this country, can in a few years raise himself to a position of great and undefined political influence. Still more disturbing is the extraordinary public indifference to such a phenomenon. Even a quarter of a century ago opinion was powerful enough to prevent any but the lesser honours going the way of the South African millionaires, and, with the exception of Rhodes, they were unable appreciably to deflect political currents by their wealth.

Lord Beaverbrook, a comparatively small man financially, has scaled heights forbidden to the great Randlords, and possesses a control of the Press which Rhodes, in the plenitude of his power, never attained. This particular ascent into Olympus may be satisfactorily explained. But the facility of the thing suggests doubts as to the quality of the largely increasing population of divinities.

EARL CURZON OF KEDLESTON

It is with a slight shock that one recalls that Lord Curzon is very nearly sixty. It used to be equally hard to realize that the Honourable George Nathaniel Curzon was not more than thirty. Mr. Curzon seemed too promising to be so young. Earl Curzon seems too promising to be so old.

There was never a stage in Lord Curzon's career in which he did not promise rather more than he has actually performed, notable though his record has been. The Honourable George Nathaniel—Nathaniel is a constantly recurring name in the family, like Benjamin among the Bathursts and Charles and Cosmo among the Gordon-Lennoxes—seems to have resembled that precocious genius of whom Captain Shandy spoke with mingled pity and disapproval. " They should have cleared it away and said nothing about it," quoth Uncle Toby, when told of an " immortal work " composed at an unnaturally early age. The peer-parson who was Lord Curzon's father seems to have acted on this sensible principle, for we have few anecdotes concerning the earliest manifestations of the future Viceroy's genius. But the doctor who assisted him into the world is said to have remarked that he had a special conformation of the head that only goes with greatness, and we know that at Eton he was a mature politician at fourteen. One admirer who remembers him there describes him as a most remarkable boy, full of beauty, vigour, and genius.

He is recalled by other contemporaries for his decided views, and the fluent energy with which he expressed them, no less than for the queer solemnity of his chubby face, the glossiness of his hats, the scrupulous neatness of his clothes, the lustre of his black hair, and his strong objection to compulsory football. He used to talk of what he would do when Prime Minister. He promised one admiring chum the post of Chancellor of the Exchequer, and nobody laughed at him for doing so.

George was not entirely happy at Eton. But there is no record of the youthful politician experiencing at school any of that rough discipline extolled as the one virtue of our higher educational system. The process of " knocking the nonsense " out of our gilded youth operates very unevenly. If the public school crushes one clever boy as a prig, it accepts another as a hero. Boys, like most barbarians, err on the side of simplicity in their judgments of exceptional people ; they have no half-way house between the Tarpeian rock and the Capitol. With the same qualities, young Curzon might have suffered torture ; as things were, he was perhaps spoiled by the reverence of his little clique. The University has more balance, and Balliol, while noting the brilliance of the Honourable George Nathaniel, was not slow to satirize his pomposity. To an undergraduate wit we owe the immortal couplet :

> " My name is George Nathaniel Curzon ;
> I am a most superior purzon."

The lines are unforgettable, chiefly because Lord Curzon has never allowed them to be forgotten.

Superiority in him is not an excrescence; it is an aroma. Like the musk in the mortar of St. Sophia at Constantinople, it is destined to last as long as the fabric. Whence Lord Curzon derives this superiority is his own secret. It may be innate. It may have been nurtured by the atmosphere of his parsonage home. In philosophy and in fact, a parson is "The Person" of his parish, and if the parson himself forgets it his sons rarely do. But when the parson is no mere Vicar of Wakefield, when he employs enough curate power to be eased of his duties without neglecting them, and when he is incidentally a Peer of the Realm, a baronet of early Stuart creation, a large landowner, and possessor of a pedigree quite genuinely traceable to the Conquest, it is not odd that the parson's son should imbibe a more than strictly necessary sense of his position.

Superiority in Lord Curzon has long been recognized as no boyish foible, but as a permanent and most important element in his character. He went round the world in a highly superior way, staying at embassies as lesser men do at hotels, presented to pagan potentates, not as an irrelevant globe-trotter, but as a statesman in training. In such books as that entertaining *Problems of the Far East* (which, I believe, Lord Curzon will not allow to be reprinted), the author reveals himself not only as a shrewd, if rather superficial, observer, but as the possessor of a quite complicated superiority, racial, social, and personal.

As Under-Secretary for Foreign Affairs, his superiority shone undimmed. The House of Commons is easily bemused with even a dexterous show of knowledge on a department of public business of which it is abysmally ignorant, and Mr. Curzon had real knowledge as well as the power of implying omniscience. It was a delight in those days to hear him explaining a concession in Persia or a mission to the Amir.

" Arthur thinks we are a vulgar lot," said Sir William Harcourt of Mr. Balfour. " George," as " Arthur " called him, was no less impressed with the mental incapacity of his audience. A tolerant and patient contempt, as of a teacher with an idiot child, was the basis of his official attitude towards the faithful Commons.

The memory of his Viceroyalty is still green in many Anglo-Indian memories. No such splendid figure had been seen in India since the days of Aurungzebe. Somebody has said that there are three ways of ruling men : by the force of arms, by the force of justice, and by the force of trumpery. Lord Curzon specialized in display. He tightened up the ceremonial paraphernalia of Calcutta and Simla to a degree that irked the honest Sedleys and Dobbins of the Civil Service and the Indian Army. " Such language was never heard west of Constantinople," grumbled General Conway, after an interview with the elder Pitt. A good many veterans who trudged through avenues of troops and officials to pay their court to the Viceroy must have felt that the West had little to learn from the East in the way of Byzantinism. There is a story that once at a church in Simla the collection bag was offered to Lord Curzon by the ordinary sidesman. The Viceroy remained blandly unconscious. Thinking it was a case of mental absorption, the sidesman gently rattled the bag. Still no sign of life on the part of the Viceroy. Then an aide-de-camp had a happy inspiration. He took the bag and offered it in due form to His Excellency, who immediately revived, and paid his due to Heaven as befitted the representative of no mean earthly majesty.

This dignity of Lord Curzon is indeed a wonderful thing. He cannot bid for a picture or a curio at Christie's without seeming to patronize Cellini or Rembrandt as well as the auctioneer. Some time ago he was one of a group of Ministers watching the American troops march through London. The others were quite human. Mr. Balfour, whom it is the fashion to call a cold philosopher, was waving a handkerchief with boyish enthusiasm. But Lord Curzon stood bolt upright, stiffly gracious, combining, like the Duke of Plaza Toro, "a pose majestic with a demeanour nobly bland," much as if he were receiving a belated but sufficient apology for the Declaration of Independence.

Just as it is not easy, in looking at an Infanta by Velasquez, to focus attention on the face, so absorbed is one in the cascade of crinolined drapery, so the mannerism of Lord Curzon does seriously increase the difficulty of a steady survey of his real qualities. We know that he is enormously clever. He would be clever if he belonged to any class, and on his social stilts even moderate intellectual stature looms up gigantesque. He has done many things brilliantly. It is less easy to say that he has attained a solid success in any one thing. Still harder is it to say that he has failed decisively and specifically. In fact, there is a good deal of mystery about the whole matter. Much difference exists in instructed opinion as to the wisdom of his policy in India. In domestic politics it is hard to place him; one can only say that he has hardly fulfilled the promise of his youth. The value of his presence in the War Cabinet is wholly unknown to the outside public. He is said to be a strong man; but so was Sir Edward Carson. We have, indeed, almost come to the stage of using the adjective "strong" when at a loss to qualify more precisely.

One quality undoubtedly he possesses in full measure. He is a master of stately and luminous speech. In this respect he has shown continuous improvement throughout his career. In other regards one is conscious of some disappointment, like that which one feels in reading *Vivian Grey*. The wonderful boy of Disraeli's sketch ends as a wonderful bore. Lord Curzon is not that; he will always remain interesting. But there is in his case, as there was in Lord Rosebery's, a feeling that a brilliant first and second act are leading up to a tame dénouement. Something may be owing to a physique never quite equal to the demands on it. More may be due to the early satisfaction of ambitions not perhaps of the highest, even in the most worldly sense. Lord Curzon is paying the penalty of a premature dignity. When he was tempted as a young man to take the Viceroyalty and its attendant honours he astonished many friends and delighted some enemies; they remembered how Atalanta lost the race through picking up a golden apple.

It may be that the explanation is altogether wider. It may be that Lord Curzon's only handicap is that he is an anachronism. Certainly he would have been temperamentally better at home in the old England of rotten boroughs and "great ladies" than in the new England of plutocracy modified by the trade union vote. His temper rather than his convictions keeps him apart from the magnates;; his convictions as well as his temper prevent him even successfully assuming any sympathy with the common man. He was probably born a hundred and fifty years too late, for his affinities are rather with the Georgians than with the Victorians. He shares their contempt for the "swinish multitude," their intense national egoism, their wonderful confidence, and perhaps a little of that quality which gave us the reputation of "perfide Albion."

A rather lonely figure, in our singular collection of war lords, he seems to typify that "ruling class" which has lost one knack of ruling without acquiring another, but retains all its passion for the toys and gauds of public life.

VISCOUNT HALDANE

THE wisdom of the ancients notwithstanding, there are few things people quarrel more furiously over than taste, and that no doubt is the reason brothers are divided, and father is estranged from son, concerning Lord Haldane. For the bland and learned Viscount is not simply a man of affairs, to be judged on his record. He is a flavour. If you like the flavour, it is exactly the flavour you like; if you dislike it, it may throw you into fits, as the smell of patchouli did Napoleon.

The Haldane cult is not a popular one. Had Lord Haldane always dissembled his love for the German classics he would still have been suspect to the great body of the English people—the present writer is not in a position to judge concerning the Scottish. Englishmen might pardon Lord Haldane's defects, but they could hardly forgive his virtues. To take one point alone, his enormous volubility, Lord Haldane offends because he talks so well, rather than because he talks so much. We are quite tolerant to men whose speeches are merely long—one might say merely Walter Long. We have no complaint against those who make demands on our time; but we do dislike those who make excessive demands on our attention. Lord Haldane has been classed as chief of bores largely because there is too much matter in his speeches, and because he pays his hearers the compliment of supposing them to be as earnest and interested as himself. Say that he is a cultivated Scotsman, with the Scottish passion for knowledge for its own sake, the Scottish logic, and the Scottish love of exhausting a subject, and you have said everything that need explain the instinctive irritation of the Southron.

The war has only intensified an existing prejudice. Other men of affairs had their spiritual homes in Germany; many were intimately connected with German families; nearly all looked eastward, like Lord Haldane, with intense admiration, slightly tinctured with fear. It was not Lord Haldane who first called the North Sea the German Ocean; one can find the name in any eighteenth-century atlas. Even if fluent command of German were a crime, Lord Haldane was not the only criminal. If a passion for the German philosophy dishonours a patriot, then most of our thinkers for a century past must plead guilty of conduct unbefitting a Briton. Coming to things more concrete, if Lord Haldane is to be condemned for believing in modern German methods, copying German legislative models, and dreaming of an "understanding" with our "cousins," then nearly all the Cabinet, most ex-Ministers, and the cream of English society should stand in the same dock for sentence. Yet it is Lord Haldane, and Lord Haldane alone, who is denounced as a stealthy pro-German and even a conscious traitor.

So stupid and so vulgar has been the outcry against the German side of Lord Haldane that even to refer to it is distasteful. Yet that German side is so important an element in the man, and has had so much influence on his career, that it cannot be ignored. It is, of course, his weaker side, as it was Carlyle's. And, as in the case of Carlyle, it is the side of which he is immoderately proud. Harvey said of Bacon, "The Lord Chancellor writes of science—like a Lord Chancellor." Bacon's successor has won fame as a metaphysician chiefly among his political and legal friends. His contributions to philosophy are rather like the poems with which Thackeray's publisher loaded his magazines, because their names carried weight in society. Nobody would ever dream of taking note of them but for the eminence of the author in another world. They give proof of a strong memory and a considerable power of comprehension; in no way do they suggest that an immortal thinker was lost through Lord Haldane's absorption in things of the moment.

One might go farther, and suggest that if Lord Haldane has ever a tendency to twaddle, it is when he engages in acts of hero-worship. A great scientist, who was also a Roman Catholic, remarked that he shut one compartment of his mind when he left the laboratory and opened another when he entered the oratory. Lord Haldane is, in the same way, two distinct beings. With a practical faculty too little recognized, he is all shrewdness and scepticism in business. But when he enters his Hegelian joss-house he seems to have little more sense of proportion than the poor Indian of the untutored mind. He talks of Kant, Goethe, and Schiller as "the men who taught mankind what was meant by the wonderful power of thought," as if Königsberg or Weimar were the Bethlehem of philosophy. Lord Haldane's excessive reverence for the great Germans is no more traitorous than the ignorant contempt of some of his critics is patriotic. But it is certainly provincial. We rightly laugh at the Sinologue who eternally thrusts on us the wisdom of Confucius because he happens to have studied that philosopher in the original. Why should we regard with submissive solemnity the enthusiasms of learned gentlemen with a fancy for Kant and Fichte? The question, like golf talk, is largely one of manners; in pushing his Germans down our throats Lord Haldane is guilty of a social solecism.

There is, too, a somewhat more serious side to the matter. Lord Haldane, with his masterful disposition, has not been content to let the German bee buzz unproductively in his own bonnet. He has always been anxious that it should make honey. In plain English he has exercised a great deal of influence over his associates, and the adoption of Prussian legislative models during the last few years has probably been due chiefly to his suggestion. For the Liberal Cabinet he was an unofficial purveyor of ideas, and all his ideas were derived either from the dead or the living "very big men" of Germany. Of his own work at the War Office—as Lord Chancellor he made little impression—it becomes us to speak, if not with gratitude, at least with respect. He made, no doubt, some mistakes. The whole credit of his achievements is not his. But when all deductions are made, there remains the great fact that, while at the beginning of the Boer War it took five weeks to despatch fifty thousand men, nearly three times that force was landed in France, without hitch or fuss, within a fortnight of the declaration of the present war. Moreover, under him was created a Territorial organization which permitted the use of battalions after two months' war training.

If Lord Haldane could be judged on this record alone he would have little reason to wince at present-day criticism or to anticipate the adverse judgment of history. But in his case there is some reason to believe that the part is greater than the whole. Haldane the man was an admirable instrument, clear-headed, industrious, indomitable. Haldane the flavour was, on the whole, probably an unfortunate influence. Of his patriotism there can at no time have been any doubt. But strong partialities must necessarily affect the judgment, and almost any counsel was better during the years preceding the war than that of a man so obsessed. It is a pity that Lord Haldane lacked the control of a master's hand. There was a strong side of him which might have been developed to even greater advantage—his business faculty and driving power in administration.

Unfortunately, the weaker side which he himself fancied fascinated also his chief, who took counsel where he should have exacted only service.

The same mistake has been made with Lord Haldane during the war. It may seem a heresy to suggest that if Mr. Asquith had had the courage to instal him at the War Office, leaving Lord Kitchener free to attend to his real duties, the result might have been more satisfactory than the muddled control of the first year of the war. But certainly that belief is shared by many who are by no means favourable to Lord Haldane on general grounds. As things are, we have made the worst of both possible Haldanes. We have deprived ourselves of his strong practical understanding and tireless energy as administrator, and we have forced into undesirable activity the pseudo-wisdom which makes him the least reliable of advisers. The only way to silence Lord Haldane is to get a bit in his mouth and set him to hard work. We have turned him loose in a forty-acre field, and he tires the very echo.

It is a nuisance, to put it no higher, to have Lord Haldane advocating schemes of education that shall be wholly German, and yet have no Germanizing tendency; to have him holding out to our working men, who know at least what they don't want, ideals founded on Kartel and Kultur models : to have him lauding the German talent for "self-organization," though a little "clear thinking" might show that the war itself is the result of the utter incapacity of the German tribes to manage their own affairs. It is merely irritating to hear from him, after some new exhibition of brutality, that the German nation, "taken in the mass," is "very like our own." But all this is only part of the price we pay for not providing Lord Haldane with a concrete job, hard enough to make him forget Göttingen.

The country does not want Lord Haldane's ideas.

It rightly suspects him as a guide. But it might
have done with him as a workman. It has gone
farther, and fared much worse.

LORD BURNHAM AND THE
" DAILY TELEGRAPH "

THE first Lord Burnham belonged to the earliest crop
of newspaper-owning peers, and his son wears the
fifteen-year-old coronet with the easy grace of a man
of pedigree. An intelligent foreigner might confuse
him with the quite new nobility. Lord Burnham
himself makes no such mistake. He is affable with
new arrivals in the House of Lords; he is affable with
everybody. But he draws a sharp line of distinction
between Edwardian and later creations. He was
greatly apprehensive of an " adulteration " of the
peerage in the unhappy Veto days, and he had decided
views on the sale of honours. One wonders what is
his real opinion of Lord Beaverbrook.

Lord Burnham's father had the honest pride of
the arrived. There was something touching in his
affection for the great newspaper he had created.
Highly creditable, too, was the interest he took in
the men who had helped him build his immense
fortune. Fame, it is true, they were denied. The
Daily Telegraph has had no " great editor," like the
Times and the *Standard*. The Levy family jealously
guarded their authority; they permitted no Mayor
of the Palace. The patriarch of Peterborough Court
showed every favour to his Eliezers. But Eliezer
had to recognize his place; he was bondservant to the
family, to young Isaac as well as to old Abraham.

The *Daily Telegraph* has thus been in an exceptional degree the reflection of a single personality.
The first Lord Burnham was exactly fitted to supply

a "long-felt want" of the later Victorian time. The
man in the street was yet unquoted. But the lower
middle-class man of the suburb and the country
town was there, and by no means satisfied either
with the price or the quality of daily papers. They
were too dear, and too narrow in their outlook.
Edward Levy, afterwards Edward Levy Lawson,
shrewdly saw his opportunity. He gave the public
a paper at the popular price of one penny, and in that
paper he printed what the public wanted. He cut
down politics, devoted great attention to the Divorce
Court, specialized on murders, systematically re-
frained from attacks on any kind of religion, and
played up to the growing taste for piquant writing
of a kind which places no strain on the intellect.

Himself of no very deep convictions, cheerful,
healthy, shrewd, content to take the commonplace
view of any subject, judging men and things from
the standpoint of material success or failure, without
ideals, but with a great deal of human sympathy, he
was precisely the man to cater for the class which
believes itself to be educated. The *Daily Telegraph*
had its early vicissitudes. It was more than once
doubtful whether it would win through the difficulties
arising from an inadequate capitalization, and quaint
stories are still told of the weekly hunt for money to
pay wages. But once the thing was well started
nothing could stop it.

The Porphyrogenitus is seldom quite equal to the
man who has battled for the purple. The present
Lord Burnham had not his father's advantages. On
the other hand he has enjoyed advantages of his own.
Eton and Balliol gave him of their best. He entered
the House of Commons when he was a mere boy, and
sat there intermittently—sometimes as a little Liberal
and sometimes as a little Conservative—until he
went to another place. He succeeded to power in
" the office " when the memory of early struggle was

very dim indeed; the newspaper was no longer a business adventure, but a family estate solid as, and vastly more profitable than, the four thousand acres on which it was the first Lord Burnham's delight to play, like Disraeli, the part of Buckinghamshire squire.

Starting with such a generous handicap, Lord Burnham, it might be imagined, could have won pretty well anything he fancied. Great political preferment was open to him. Or he could, if he pleased, satisfy a purer and perhaps more useful ambition. Assured of a prodigious income from his established success, he could have done something not merely for English journalism but for English literature. He could have helped, by a judicious and possibly not unprofitable expenditure, to remove a great reproach. The barrenness of English thought during the last thirty years is not accidental. It arises partly from the conviction of British publishers that no book which is hard to read will yield a profit, and possibly even more from the complete indifference of British Governments to any intellectual considerations. Even in the humble matter of translation our record is deplorable. It is a fact that before the present war the works of Treitschke could only be studied in the original, or in a foreign medium. True, Treitschke was not inherently worth much notice, but in the peculiar circumstances it might be thought that it was somebody's business to bring this dreamer of unpleasantly practical dreams to the attention of the people he threatened. There is scarcely a limit to the good a thinking man with Lord Burnham's ample means could have effected in half a dozen directions.

Lord Burnham, however, has been content to carry on. He has not cut the shop. He is greatly interested in it—as a shop. The advertisement columns of the *Daily Telegraph* seem to be his special care. Paper shortage notwithstanding, the Bloomsbury boarding-house can still advertise its inexpensive inclusive terms, the cultivated family in Tooting can still disclose its yearnings for the society of a refined paying guest, and the owner of a smart governess cart for which the owner has no further use owing to the war can still reach the middle-aged lady who wants one to suit her cob of 14·1. But when we turn to the editorial columns we find little light or leading. I remember once going through the file of *Galignani's Messenger* for the Hundred Days. It had been very severe on Napoleon after the abdication; it was very severe on him after Waterloo; but during the Hundred Days its leading articles were on all kinds of queer things—the favourite perfumes of Ninon de Lenclos and the wonders of the Alhambra —quite unconnected with affairs in France.

The *Daily Telegraph* for some years, and especially since the war, has given the same impression of embarrassed irrelevance. It may consciously steer for nowhere. It certainly gets there. There are a few subjects on which it still speaks with a certain voice. It is all for national unity, which it would appear is to be attained by agreeing, say, that Mr. Hayes Fisher is indispensable. It is always ready to enlarge dithyrambically on the glory of France, or the glory of Serbia, or the glory of the British Navy, or any kind of glory. It makes at regular intervals the discovery that " His Majesty was never nearer the hearts of the people than when," etc. But all these things get us no forwarder, nor, it must be confessed, do the *Daily Telegraph's* dissections of Lord Lansdowne's contributions to its post-bag.

It is, in fact, becoming increasingly difficult to find what class of man derives stimulus from Lord Burnham's editorial direction. The paper is still the oracle of the boarding-houses, and, perhaps *propter hoc*, is invariably the one London journal which the visiting foreigner reads. By old habit, if for no better reason, a number of suburban and country families continue to take it in. Even in these days of paper famine it still has a decided advantage in bulk; its usefulness for wrapping things in, and putting under the carpets, recommends it to economical households. But what special kind of intellectual hunger it satisfies is less easy to discover. The theatre-goer has got beyond the simple standards of Clement Scott, but the *Daily Telegraph* has not. Few serious-minded men care anything about the kind of politics it professes. Its literary tastes are too ingenuous for the new generation. Its facetious reporters fail to cheer with their lumbering gaiety. There is only a languid echo of the buoyant vulgarity of its early days. It was said of the Bourbons that they forgot nothing and learned nothing. It may be said of the *Daily Telegraph* that it has learned little and forgotten much.

Still it prospers amazingly. There is often more profit in selling ready-made and partly worn-out things than in supplying a more dignified need. Few trades are more prosperous than that of the old clothes dealer in a really big way. The continued commercial success of the *Daily Telegraph* would seem to suggest that cast-off ideas yield as handsome a profit as cast-off garments. The paper may be little more to Lord Burnham than a property, but it is a very handsome property. And, after all, an old clothes shop is a very useful institution. Mr. Isaac Moses is probably fulfilling a more vital social function than many professed philanthropists, and Lord Burnham may have his uses in supplying those who are permanently hard-up in an intellectual sense. At any rate, he does uncommonly well out of the business.

MR. W. M. HUGHES

THIRTY-FOUR years ago two young men stood on London Bridge, as Tom Pinch and his sister once did, watching the boats. One of them need not concern us. The other concerns us a good deal.

He had been born some twenty years before in South Wales, but had lived nearly all his life in London. Educated at the Baroness Burdett-Coutts Foundation School in Westminster, he knew the greyer life of a region in which social contrasts are perhaps as violent as in any part of London. Mr. William Morris Hughes has told us that as a lad he was often engaged in fighting the Wesleyan boys in the Horseferry Road, and that he once won a prize for French : a tongue not easily acquired, it might be imagined, in such an institution as that which served him as Alma Mater. It may be fairly inferred, from these facts, that young Hughes was quick and of a combative temperament. Probably he had also some capacity for reflection, and it is easy to picture him musing on such monuments of the past as Westminster Hall, the Abbey, and Westminster School, as well as on evidences of the present, like the rookeries off the Horseferry Road and the old Millbank Prison.

How would London, as he saw it, strike the sharp Welsh lad, with all sorts of vague ambitions stirring within him? For him all the higher things would be represented by stone. The Abbey would stand for a petrified religion ; Westminster Hall would typify the sterile antiquities of an obsolete constitution ; Westminster School would remind him that such as he could expect nothing from what was once specially designed for his like. Here were clergy with their antique prayer mills, politicians with their hoary platitudes, schoolmasters with their scraps of Latin and Greek syntax, and good form and the other things that go to make a gentleman—all entirely oblivious of the real needs of the living London and the living England. And there were the packed slums in which every vice grew rank and every virtue took some distorted form. That was what lay behind the lad as he looked over the bridge.

Before young Hughes lay the water path to " the Colonies," what are now called, in a politely embarrassed way, the Oversea States. In England, apart from some unusual luck or very adroit dishonesty, he could hope for nothing more than a living; in the Colonies there was slightly more chance of going under, but considerably more chance of coming to the top. Hughes and his friend, looking at the steamboats, suddenly decided to take one. They packed up and went to Australia. There followed the usual confused attempts to fashion something tolerable out of the void. Hughes tended stock, took jobs on coasting craft, did a little mining, did a little of everything, until he found his niche as trade union official, agitator, Labour Member, and the rest of it. His early combativeness developed. Instead of fighting Wesleyans, he attacked monopolists. His talent for picking up information grew with enlarged circumstances. He picked up law as he had picked up French, became a barrister, and acquired a good grip of Australian public questions. Ten years only had elapsed from the Hughes Hegira before he had reached the position of a prominent member of the New South Wales Parliament. When Australian unity became a fact, he was among the first elected to the Commonwealth Legislature.

That is how " the Colonies " take hold of our surplus raw material, and work it up for their own purposes. Or, rather, that is how, in a free atmosphere, men of talent grow in the measure of their capacities, their virtues, and it may be of their vices.

It would be pleasant to leave Mr. Hughes arrived at a
deserved eminence, a man to adorn any Colonial tale,
and to point the moral of the losses we suffer by the
emigration of discouraged young ambition.   Unfortunately, events have conspired to make it impossible
to consider the Prime Minister of Australia solely in
the Smiles spirit, as a bright example of self-help. He
has partly been forced, but has also partly chosen, to
come into violent contact with things not purely Australian, and it is that part of his activities which is
necessarily more vividly impressed upon us than his
wholly admirable record in the Antipodes.

In 1915 Mr. Hughes visited this country. He knew
very little of English life, but he had his early
memories, which sufficed to give him a just contempt
for many of our institutions, but also a most unjust
notion of the real qualities of the nation. He either
did not know, or had forgotten, that our old and
polished society breeds in great numbers persons
who are described by the police as confidence men.
Scotland Yard takes cognisance only of the coarser
varieties of the class. It affects to know nothing of
those who infest political society, lying in wait for
innocents from overseas and the provinces.   Mr.
Hughes's first speech had much the same effect on
these gentlemen that the appearance of a stout Suffolk
farmer might on a roomful of professional " crooks."
He found himself surrounded with persons flashing
great wads of Bank of Patriotism notes, which he,
poor man! could not possibly detect as spurious.
Before honest Mr. Hughes well knew what he was
doing, he was hocussed, and he has not yet succeeded
in throwing off the influence of the drugs.

It suited the political purposes of a certain clique
to represent Mr. Hughes as the one earnest man
struggling to free the British Commonwealth from
German influences, but frustrated in that endeavour
by a knot of English party politicians. Broadly

speaking, this clique, of all others, was most naturally
hostile to every ideal Mr. Hughes stood for in Australian politics. It desired Protection in the interests
of British landlords and manufacturers, and not, as in
Australia's case, in the interests of the workers. It
stood for a kind of Imperialism which, in the long run,
must have come into collision with the quite natural
desire of Australia to become more and more a distinct
nation. It stood for minority rule both in Great
Britain and in Ireland. It had been, as much as any
party—there is really little degree of guilt—responsible
for the stagnation which young Hughes of the Horseferry Road had found intolerable. But it found in
the fervour of the maturer Hughes a weapon which it
could use, and that weapon was used without scruple.

Mr. Hughes as an Australian statesman must be left
to the judgment of Australia. Australia has declined
twice to pass a mandate for conscription at his invitation—some add because of his invitation—and it is
whispered with some assurance that the Prime Minister
is not precisely anxious to terminate his present visit
to London. It is pointed out by Australian critics that
the great work which he claims credit for, "cutting
the tentacles of the great metal octopus," etc., was
merely a matter of official routine; contracts with
German firms had necessarily to be broken when war
came. There is, in fact, no evidence from the Antipodes that Mr. Hughes is regarded as a man of very
exceptional calibre, and it is pretty well known that he
retains office chiefly because it is undesirable to complicate the political position.

Still, Mr. Hughes is an Australian, and Australia
would no doubt be with him in any serious collision
with British opinion. It is that possibility which
makes so exceedingly serious the transformation of a
Dominion Prime Minister into a British party asset.
The formal relations of Australia, or any other
Dominion, to the Mother Country, are of less import-

ance than many people imagine. It really does not matter very much whether we continue to send second-rate noblemen to represent the King in the Commonwealth. What does matter is that there shall be no sense of grievance or incompatibility between the two communities, that Australia shall have no feeling of being used by Britain, and that Britain shall be free from any impression of being bustled or hustled by Australia.

It would be unfair to accuse Mr. Hughes of consciously imperilling a good understanding. He has "butted in," to adopt Mr. Lloyd George's Americanism, with the best intentions. He believes "butting in " is really appreciated by the mass of people in this country. He is, indeed, a man singularly ingenuous. He does not seem to have suspected in the least the very suspicious people who have " run " him in London ; he does not appear even to be conscious of being " run." He has a good many points in common with our own Prime Minister. He makes it a rule never to see more than one side of a case at a time, though he may see all sides in turn. He is more the slave than the master of his own rhetoric. His eloquence has not the same poetic quality as Mr. Lloyd George's ; he lacks the unerring instinct for effect which make even Mr. George's most commonplace efforts distinctive. He seldom coins a phrase ; his figures come from the till and not from the mint, and mainly belong to the copper currency. But he has something of the same power of reaching the ordinary man, and not a little of the same habit of intoxicating himself as well as his audience.

Such a man may be useful if his energies are properly controlled and applied to a suitable objective. He may easily become a calamitous nuisance if he runs amuck, and Mr. Hughes has, in fact, rather run amuck during both his visits to Great Britain. It cannot be a good thing to permit any considerable

party in the United Kingdom to believe that they have
a determined enemy in the Prime Minister of an
Overseas Dominion. Nor can it be for the benefit of
the Alliance as a whole that Mr. Hughes should
declaim at this time a Monroe Doctrine for the Pacific.
Strangely enough, the world at large is no more
interested in the special Australian point of view than
it is in the special Montenegrin point of view. We
cannot blame Mr. Hughes for failing to see things in
their exact proportion; there were British propa-
gandists who once believed that France and Russia,
Italy and the United States, were enormously interested in the bombing of Broadstairs and the shelling
of Hartlepool.

But it is a fact that the world thinks very little of
New Guinea and Samoa, and a great deal about the
avoidance of further dispute about such trifles as
Samoa and New Guinea. Monroe Doctrines of any
kind belong, like spheres of influence and places in the
sun, to the old world which has perished in this war.
Mr. Hughes, with all his progressive notions, seems
too old-fashioned even to conceive what the new world
must be if it is to be a world worth living in. The
idea behind the League of Nations is, indeed, still
generally misunderstood. That League does not
threaten German Imperialism alone, but all Im-
perialisms. If it aimed simply at fixing for ever the
status arrived at after the war it would be only another
Holy Alliance, an instrument of oppression which
could as easily be used for purposes of industrial
slavery as for the destruction of nationalism. It would
seem that Mr. Hughes envisages a world in which
what is called Anglo-Saxondom will be all-powerful.
That may be very pleasing to " Anglo-Saxon " racial
pride. Have we the smallest guarantee that the rest
of the world—a not inconsiderable fragment—will be
content?

The Pacific Monroe Doctrine will be useless if the

new order comes. If that vision fails to materialize the Pacific Monroe Doctrine will have, like many more important questions, to be the subject of much huckstering on the old plan. In any case, insistence on it at the present moment can be of no possible benefit and may be a real disadvantage. It would, of course, be calamitous to suggest to the Dominions that their sacrifices will not entitle them to a voice, and a powerful one, in the settlement. It is equally out of the question that the demands of France, Italy, and Belgium shall be passed over. But just as there is unwisdom in wrangling over Continental claims in the presence of an enemy watching for any opportunity to create divisions among the Allies, so there is a very practical inconvenience in the shouted discussion of those details which Mr. Hughes has naturally so much at heart.

Let us win the war, and all these things—or things much better—will be added to us. But the main aim will not be advanced by a furious quarrel between one of the British political parties and the Premier of the Australian Commonwealth. That is why many people who have sympathy and admiration for Mr. Hughes entertain misgivings which they hardly dare express. For the position is not a little awkward. It is never pleasant to give a hint to a guest, and there is here the added danger that it might be construed into an affront to a nation.

SIR AUCKLAND GEDDES

THERE are some Ministers who are distrusted chiefly
because they are known, and others who are little
known and much trusted. To the latter fortunate
category Sir Auckland Geddes belonged until quite
recently.

The Geddes myth is a curious example of the
growth of legend in an age when ninety-nine people
out of a hundred must base their impressions on
printed matter. The general public is quite without
means of estimating the true merits of the Geddes
brothers. It knows, on the whole, about as much
about them as of Hengist and Horsa. Yet for months
it went on chanting with Islamic simplicity, " Brainy
is Eric, and Auckland is his brother." No doubt the
legend has some foundation in fact. There are some,
in the War Cabinet or elsewhere, who did actually
know how far Sir Eric Geddes is an inspired First
Lord, and in what degree Sir Auckland Geddes has
succeeded as Minister of National Service. But the
million to whom the efficiency of the Geddes brothers
was an article of faith were, like the Athenians of old,
performing an act of worship to an unknown god.

The case of our present subject is more remarkable
than that of Sir Eric, who was obviously an excellent
railwayman if nothing else. In the earlier career of
Sir Auckland Geddes we search in vain for any
illumination. Those biographers who are always
ready to discern evidence of precocious talent in men
who arrive have, of course, done their best in his case.
We are told that young Geddes's speeches at the
Edinburgh Union left an abiding impression on all
who heard them. He enchanted his friends with his
acute comments on men and things. There was
something in his long, gaunt face men could never

forget. His "keen eyes," we are told, as if it were something to admire, "flashed from cavernous hollows at every passing stranger." As a strong Tory, he was a terrible antagonist for Mr. Hogge, now M.P., who led the Liberals. It seemed to his admiring intimates that he had only to choose from a dozen brilliant careers. He might even become a Sherlock Holmes of real life. But all this youthful prestige did not save him from settling down into a mild assistant anatomical demonstrator.

After some years of humdrum, broken by service in South Africa, Geddes went to Canada as a Professor of Anatomy in the McGill University. This not specially adventurous enterprise is described as "obeying the call of the wild"—Montreal being a notoriously unsettled place. There was a slightly higher salary and increased social position, but the post was quite in keeping with the mediocrity that had preceded it. In fact, the cold, inexorable truth is that if Geddes were an extraordinary man, his career was, until the outbreak of war, about as far from extraordinary as could well be. There is not, and never was, a lack of young men combining an average professional knowledge with a capacity of making debating society speeches and impressing their friends as deep thinkers.

At the beginning of the war Auckland Geddes, like many others, enlisted as a private, and quickly rose to commissioned rank. Then occurred a series of accidents which brought him amazingly rapid promotion. In 1915 he was at General Headquarters "doing casualties." It was a complicated business, as the Army then did it, but not inherently more troublesome than the arrangements by which the headquarters of a teashop business keeps in touch with the requirements of its branches. Auckland Geddes, bringing a new mind to the problem, suggested simplifications which commended themselves to his superiors. The British military mind knows no half-measures. It either breaks a man for showing intelligence, or reverences him as a prodigy. Geddes had luck. Instead of being snubbed, he was made a Major and put in charge of the casualties department.

That brought him in direct contact with Lord Derby, who was then in the midst of his recruiting campaign, and desired accurate information regarding the wastage of war. It is easy to understand how greatly the noble Earl was impressed by the clarity of Major Geddes's intellect. The two men were obviously made for each other. On the one hand was Lord Derby, with sixty thousand acres and a slightly flustered understanding; on the other, Major Geddes, with twopence-halfpenny and an uncanny knowledge of all sorts of mysterious things; he probably even understood logarithms. Why was such a man wasted in France? Lord Derby, perhaps with no unselfish view, took immediate steps to secure the paragon, and Auckland Geddes started on the higher plane as Assistant Recruiter-General, and, in unofficial language, as Lord Derby's headpiece.

He marched steadily from triumph to triumph. He " did well," as the phrase goes, as Assistant; he " did well " as Director-General; he " did well " when set to reorganize the National Service Department, where poor Mr. Neville Chamberlain had " done " so badly. It is easier to ask than to define in what " doing well " consists. It seems probable, however, that Sir Auckland Geddes does really possess what, compared with the organ of the average soldier, politician, and business man, is an orderly mind. He knows how to use his own intelligence and, what is more important, the intelligence of his subordinates. He does not altogether lose himself in an infinity of detail. He has that saving touch of indolence which, in association with brains and a capacity for concentrated effort on occasion, helps a man of affairs to master his job, instead of becoming its slave. His set speeches, of course, prove nothing. These things do not emerge, in a sort of Minerva-birth, from the brain of a Front Bench Jove, but are the work of a whole department licked into shape by one of the brighter members of the great Barnacle family. But there is a certain quality in all his utterances which suggests that he has the gift of getting to the heart of the matter. One feels instinctively that when he confuses an issue the fault is not with his brain.

It has been mentioned that Sir Auckland's chief business in the Army was to deal with casualties; in other words, with dead or partly dead men. His business in professional life was anatomy, also concerned with things dead or doomed. The habit of years is not easily broken, and the chief reason why Sir Auckland, after many months of constantly ascending reputation, began to accumulate unpopularity appears to be that, in his new office, he dealt with living men rather in the spirit in which he totalled up corpses in the Adjutant-General's Department, or dissected "subjects" in Edinburgh and Montreal. In addition to the insensitive imagination of youth and the callousness of the soldier, there is the adamantine hardness of a certain professorial type. His lack of sympathy is rather phenomenal, and, to do him justice, he does not assume the pose of humanity. Under him the National Service Department has worked with the smoothness of a machine, but also with its indiscriminating ruthlessness. He sees no disadvantage in using mahogany for packing-cases, employing razors to chop wood, or upsetting the whole structure of society in order to get a few extra thousands of invalid recruits. He admits no hardship. "Look at me," he says, in effect, when criticized, "I have suffered all for my country; I gave up my comfortable appointment, served as a private; and supported injuries which unfit me for

further military service. The case of a father of ten
is hard, no doubt, but then war is a hard business."
Unfortunately he has not always helped to make it
less hard. There is no record, for example, of his
interfering to check the unfeeling levity with which
National Service representatives have often jeered at
unfortunate men before the tribunals. What does it
matter about people's feelings? The main thing is
to get the men; whether a man goes into the Army
sadly but with resignation, or whether he goes in
embittered by a sense of insult and injustice, is of
less moment.

But the main count against Sir Auckland Geddes is
more serious than that of insensibility. "He is a
beast, but he is a just beast," said the schoolboy of
the master who flogged him. In the case of the higher
age men, on which Sir Auckland came in conflict
with public opinion, the complaint was not so much
of severity as of injustice. The Act was passed on a
definite understanding which was afterwards ignored.
Sir Auckland Geddes, taxed with the matter, faced
his critics with a hauteur to which men of the calibre
of some of them were not accustomed. It was unfortunate for the Geddes myth that he took this course.
No people is so tolerant of incapacity, or even of dishonesty, as the English. They bear with astonishing
patience the revelation of supreme imbecility in their
rulers. They make the most liberal allowance for
unredeemed pledges, and are always ready to listen
indulgently to a " personal explanation," even though
it is merely a confession of what is now called "indelicate " conduct. But they do not like being bullied,
and Sir Auckland Geddes, in an evil hour for his
repute, decided to bully.

With that the myth came to an end. It could not
survive the apology which Sir Auckland was forced
to make to Sir Donald Maclean, or rather to what
Sir Donald Maclean courageously and eloquently

represented—the outraged sense of justice of the
English people. Sir Auckland Geddes may, if he is
wise, still occupy a position of influence and public
usefulness; but he is evidently obsolete in the capacity
of superman. He will in future have to justify his
policy and account for his undertakings in the usual
way, instead of relying on the brilliance of a career
in regard to which it is still difficult to apportion
exactly the elements of merit and good fortune.

MR. H. A. L. FISHER

WHEN Mr. Lloyd George formed his " Business
Government " there was one appointment, and perhaps one only, which offended nobody and pleased all
who thought they understood its meaning and inten-
tion. It was that of Mr. Herbert Albert Laurens
Fisher, Vice-Chancellor of Sheffield University, as
Minister of Education.

Undeniably this was the happiest of the " expert "
appointments. Mr. Fisher suffered none of the handicaps of the ordinary " practical " man suddenly called
on to save his country. He had no deep-seated anti-
social instinct to overcome. He had never known
what it was to grind an axe. He could be suspected
of no mean personal ambitions. He knew his business
very much better than the swollen millionaire generally
knows the trade which yields his wealth, but not the
faintest suspicion of selfish interest could attach to
him. Besides, it was quite without precedent that an
Education Minister should know aught about education. Ever since there had been an Education
Department it had been the refuge either of the dullest
or the least influential of party men. Sometimes it
was the reward of an excessively stupid person with
" claims." Occasionally it was given to a rattling

platform speaker, not considered worth the higher dignity of five thousand a year. Now and again it was used to provide a place for some silent and diffident man who happened to be a useful intellectual asset to a showy but very unsound team. Mr. Lloyd George, with his instinct for effect, saw the advantage of making a break from tradition in this office of all others. With all his apparent defiance of convention, he was under irresistible compulsion to placate the Quirites while tickling the ears of the Plebs. In focussing attention on Mr. Fisher he made people forget Lord Derby.

Mr. Fisher's comparative youth—he is still only fifty-three—was not his least recommendation. He had escaped the worst effects of the " Teutonic " epidemic of Victorian days. If he once had spiritual lodgings at Göttingen, he did not, like Lord Haldane, look back on them as his home. His German culture struck no deeper than that which he imbibed in Paris. He returned to England, indeed, with a saner view of European things than that of almost any scholar of his time. There is no trace of German pedantry in his admirable studies of the Napoleonic period and his *Republican Tradition in Europe.* The triumph of the pickelhaube in 1870 was distant enough not to disturb a judgment which, left to itself, was sound. He did not share the belief, so common among intelligent Englishmen a little before his day, and almost universal among stupid Englishmen till quite lately, that the country of Turenne does not know how to fight or the country of Richelieu how to rule. In a word, few British scholars were freer from that intellectual snobbery which allowed the accident of a political and dynastic connection to colour its whole scheme of thought. Mr. Fisher had shown himself a Liberal in the true sense, both in his general outlook on affairs and in his own special province. His own mind enriched with the best that Winchester and

Oxford could give him, he had a far livelier sense of modern needs than most representatives of the older culture, and had shown an enthusiasm for general education in pleasing contrast with the grudging and monopolistic spirit that still distinguishes the Universities and public schools, which the rich long ago captured from the poor.

These positive recommendations, and the important negative one of being free from sectarian bitterness, caused the few disinterested enthusiasts for education in this country to believe that the time had come, and also the man. We might, under the wise rule of Mr. Fisher, actually become an educated people; there was hope even for the upper classes. And, above all, the education might possibly have a real national flavour. We might give up the idea of fighting Germany with her own weapons, and set up an intellectual Essen of our own. People who remembered with a blush that, apart from Darwin, a physicist or two, a few economists, and the mechanicians, all British thought during the last hundred and fifty years had been borrowed from Germany began to hope for a revival of the great tradition of the seventeenth century, when the Continent turned in reverence to a brilliant succession of British philosophers.

One fear mingled with these hopes. It was that Mr. Fisher, with all his knowledge and enthusiasm, might fail through unfamiliarity with the ways of the House of Commons. It is curious that, while quite legitimate expectations have been somewhat disappointed, this equally rational misgiving has proved even more illusory. Mr. Fisher proved from the first a natural master of the Parliamentary manner. Aided by a handsome and winning presence, and a style of speech which impresses by its distinction, but does not offend by a too donnish quality, he gained the ear of the House of Commons in his maiden effort, and has never lost it. Further, he has quickly acquired

the still more difficult art of " managing " that curious
assembly. Mr. Asquith himself must have admired
the consistent skill with which the former Oxford tutor
has steered his craft, whether on the swelling tide of
a Second Reading debate or through the shallows and
miseries of Committee.

This might seem the highest praise and the most
complete justification for the Prime Minister's choice.
So indeed it may be, from a Prime Minister's standpoint. But to the earnest outsider the matter presents
itself quite otherwise. So far as he has failed in his
great task, Mr. Fisher's failure is due to that
Parliamentary tact on which he has been lavishly
complimented. He went forth to fight with beasts at
Ephesus. He ended by mastering the wild beasts in
something the same sense that a Zoo attendant is their
lord, as a sort of Hagenbeck who cannot quell his
man-eaters, but only confines them behind a Mappin
terrace. It might be dexterous; it was hardly heroic.

Mr. Fisher, it will be remembered, started out with
two main ideas. One was that education should be
continuous to the age of eighteen, the other that the
horrible system of child labour should cease. Lancashire, which has been accurately described as the
Ulster of the education question, at once mobilized
against the abolition of half-time. But Lancashire
expressed itself as reasonable. It did recognize some
necessity for advance, and put forward a counter-
proposal to Mr. Fisher's original plan of 320 hours'
education a year for boys and girls between the ages
of fourteen and eighteen. Instead it suggested half-
time between the ages of fourteen and sixteen.

Mr. Fisher had probably an opportunity of com-
promising on somewhat better terms than these. At
any rate, he could have closed with a bargain which
many will think possessed certain advantages over his
original idea. Instead he proposed an arrangement
which not only reduced the age limit, but reduced the

hours of instruction as well. It was not a matter of accepting half a loaf as better than no bread, but of preferring half a loaf to three-quarters. "We will give you half the week up to sixteen," said Lancashire. "Certainly not," replied the Minister of Education, with much severity. "For seven years you may have your way as to the age limit, and I will have my way as to the number of hours given to education. They shall not be twenty odd hours a week, as you propose, but only seven."

This singular proceeding has been represented as dictated by anxiety not to give statutory sanction to the principle of half-time, the said principle being apparently more objectionable than the plain fact of three-quarters or seven-eighths time. Tempting as it is, one need not stop to consider this remarkable argument. For most education enthusiasts the main and very unpleasing fact was that there had been a surrender, and a grave one, to vested interest. The real interest of the nation and its youth had been sacrificed to the fancied interest of a number of rich men. One can pardon in comparison the short-sighted greed of many poor parents who are not sufficiently enlightened to grasp the lesson which the abounding prosperity of the United States should have taught them—that the broadest and surest foundations of a nation's material well-being are the mental and physical vigour of its masses.

The Bill made its progress to the Statute Book over the wreckage of most of the hopes which Mr. Fisher's appointment had created. He had not mastered Parliament. Parliament had subdued him. On the whole it would have been better to have gone down on the field than to have signed such a capitulation.

The moral would seem to be that no true reform can be expected in any direction, however honest and able the reformer, until a wholly different atmosphere reigns at Westminster. The lump is not to be affected by a little leaven of sincere purpose; leaven is for the good bread, and this lump is mostly of mere sawdust, the débris of all sorts of dead matter. Until the elector insists on representatives who do represent, all our St. Georges will suffer one of two fates—the Dragon of sectional selfishness will breakfast on them if they quit themselves in wholly knightly and saintly fashion, or they will end by breakfasting with the Dragon, who has generally friends in the quarters where breakfasts are given. The sadder of the two fates seems to have befallen that once very perfect knight, Mr. H. A. L. Fisher.

SIR MARK SYKES

PRAED'S observation that "the Whigs are wicked knaves, and very like the Tories," can only be accepted with qualification. Certainly there is no very vivid contrast between the rank and file of both great parties. Between the well-born cadet, the pushing lawyer, the astute company promoter, the honour-hungry tradesman, and the adventurer of doubtful blood, who sit on the Unionist benches, and their counterparts on whom the Liberal Whip may always depend, there is no difference discernible by the unaided senses. But there are still men of whom one can say "This is and always will be a Liberal," and "No power on earth can make this man other than a Tory."

Sir Mark Sykes is a Tory. His, however, is not just the Toryism that goes naturally with a fairly old baronetcy, a much older gentility, and £80,000 or so a year. He would be a Tory equally if he were struggling at the Bar or writing for his bread. Nor is it that narrow and ungenerous obstructiveness which has passed for Toryism since about the time the

party dropped its fine old name and began to call itself
Conservative.   Still less has it affinity with the
specific negation implied in the modern " Unionist "
label.   Sir Mark's Toryism is of an older and healthier
school.   Quite modern in appurtenances, he belongs
to a very ancient company.   He would have been at
home in the " country party " of Stuart days, among
men ready to die for the King, but quite ready also
to speak plainly to his Majesty on occasion, equally
impatient of Dutch intriguers and French mistresses,
and hating impartially courtiers and professional
patriots.   Macaulay has taught the ordinary Englishman to look on old Toryism as a slavish and irrational
creed.   Yet the Tory more nearly represented the
average mind of Stuart England than did Somers or
Montagu, and it is not without significance that even
to-day the working man, while placing the mere Conservative and the Liberal on much the same level,
often betrays a real kindness for the honest " back-
woodsman."   Lord Willoughby de Broke will get an
amused and even sympathetic hearing from audiences
which would howl down a more "serious " politician.

Sir Mark Sykes is, of course, a very different person
from Lord Willoughby.   Indeed, he is one of the few
men on the back benches of whom it can be said that
he arrests notice whenever he breaks silence.   He
combines a very active and acute intelligence with
a considerable gift of expression.   He has not yet
attained in the spoken word that admirable style
which makes his books of travel so eminently readable.
Perhaps he has not yet taken political speaking seriously enough.   But he never degenerates into slovenly
expression or loose periphrasis, and when a subject
moves him he rises to a sober and impressive eloquence.   He has, too, real knowledge of a variety of
subjects.   His life has been largely spent in travel,
and he has far more than the adventurous globe-
trotter's familiarity with the Near East.

Nor is he, like so many travelled Englishmen, merely interested in old savageries and brand-new civilizations. It was a common fault of our young plutocrats that, while they had hunted big game in every wilderness, they knew no more of Europe than its big hotels and gambling houses. Sir Mark Sykes has an advantage which the English Roman Catholic often possesses over the ordinary pagan man of family. He has not been allowed to forget that he is a European as well as an Englishman. He had imbibed some of the culture of Latin Europe before he went to Cambridge. What precisely they taught at Monaco and Brussels we need not enquire, but it was obviously something that is not learned at Portadown—or even at Trinity College, Dublin.

The mention of Portadown brings one to the quarrel of an English Tory with the Ulster-ridden Unionist Party. Sir Mark Sykes is no Home Ruler in the ordinary sense; he is of the new Federationist school. But he recognizes two sufficiently obvious facts which the great majority of his party have never had the candour to face. The first is that there is an Irish question; that Ireland is not a collection of English counties, but a nation, and not altogether a small one. The second is that Sir Edward Carson's position is neither logically nor morally to be distinguished from that of the leaders of the Sinn Fein party. He has had the courage, not once, but many times, to call a spade a spade, and Sir Edward Carson an incendiary. This may not argue any great audacity on the part of a man far beyond the reach of arguments ordinarily powerful enough to stifle independence. But there are some scores of men equally fortunate in their worldly affairs who must have thought the same thing, and have failed to say it.

Possibly this refusal to bow the knee to the Ulster chieftain may partially explain the fact that the most talented private member on the Unionist benches, though, I believe, offered some minor Ministerial post, has never been regarded as eligible for high office. But insubordination is not the only weakness of Sir Mark Sykes. He is afflicted with a sense of humour, and has even been known to lampoon his leaders. He is understood not to regard Mr. Bonar Law with any great reverence, and has never schooled himself to speak with due solemnity of Sir F. E. Smith. Nothing is more fatal to a young member of the House of Commons than a reputation for undisciplined brilliance, and the habit of caricaturing his seniors may have seriously affected Sir Mark Sykes's prospects. But it is also quite possible that he himself prefers for the present the liberty of a private member. Those who know him best credit him with large ambitions, which, however, he can wait to satisfy.

However that may be, this healthy, wealthy, and still comparatively young Yorkshireman cannot be left out of account in any estimate of the political future. Nobody can foresee what is to emerge from the present welter. Official Liberal and official Conservative are about equally discredited. "Business" members have, on the whole, disappointed expectations. They were to be strong, silent men, who would do miracles by stealth and blush to find them fame. Instead they have mostly proved excellent talkers and wretched performers, skilled in making messes and dexterous in explaining them away. Labour has thrown up one or two moderately efficient administrators, but several lamentable failures. Generally speaking, its record is not brilliant; its "machine" is, moreover, in the hands of men by no means generally trusted. It may be fairly anticipated that there will be a more democratic tendency in the politics of the immediate future. But "democracy" does not necessarily mean the rule of Mr. Henderson and Mr. Ramsay MacDonald. It is just possible that "the people," which is not quite the same thing as organized labour, may take a line of its own.

If it does, there is no real reason why the Toryism represented by Sir Mark Sykes should not regain a good deal of the support which Unionism of recent years has lost. After the war England will in all probability exert far greater influence in politics than she has done of late years; one seems already to smell revolt against Scottish, Irish, and Welsh domination. But England is temperamentally Tory, and never more Tory than when in a Radical mood. Cobbett, always looking backward with satisfaction, round him with anger, and forward with gloom, was the concrete expression of that paradox. Conservatism of the kind the present generation has been accustomed to is either doomed to impotence or is destined to tease and worry the country into revolution. But an English Tory who recognizes, as Sir Mark Sykes does, that many a man desires Mr. Outhwaite's land policy who detests Mr. Outhwaite's views on all else, might do much to guide the torrent of innovation into safe channels. Is the member for Central Hull heavy metal enough for such a rôle?

LORD BUCKMASTER OF CHEDDINGTON

LORD BUCKMASTER, still in what is now counted early middle age, nourishes a competent physique and a sufficient understanding on the pension of an ex-Lord Chancellor of England. How it happened is worth recalling, and perhaps the best way is to begin, Smiles fashion, at the beginning.

There was nothing in the early circumstances of Stanley Owen Buckmaster to suggest that he would arrive at the highest legal dignity at an age when many able advocates are wondering whether they can afford the luxury of silk. His origin was comfortable, but not distinguished. The son of a member of the staff of the Science and Art Department at South Kensington, he was given a good education, took his degree at Christ Church, and entered on his studies of the law at the Inner Temple, where he received his call in 1884. The Bar is described as a great lottery, and certainly its chief prizes are rather capriciously distributed. But, after all, it is very much like other professions in being, on the whole, kind to the pertinacious man of moderate abilities. A genius may quite likely be starved into despair, driven to drink, or diverted into journalism by the weariness of waiting and the drudgery of small beginnings. A diffident man, a lazy man, or a man of inconveniently large sympathies is likely to be still complaining after ten years that it is impossible to pay for chambers and laundress out of professional income. But steady work, helped by a prosaic temperament and some faculty of discreet self-advertisement, generally tells. It told in the case of Mr. Stanley Buckmaster. Seventeen years of assiduous application placed him in a position to take silk and look round for a seat in Parliament.

He had long been marked by the Liberal caucus as a promising candidate, and he came in for Cambridge on the great tidal wave of 1906. He failed to hold the constituency four years later, but had meanwhile established "claims," and was allotted at the first opportunity the safe seat of Keighley. His reputation at the Bar was rather high, but purely professional; it has never been pretended that he was either a great advocate or a profound lawyer, but he was keen, dependable, and neat in his presentation of an argument. In politics the same character attached to him. He never coined a phrase of note or forsook the safe path of official Liberalism. But he had learned faultlessly the party brief, never gave him-

self away, and made himself agreeable in the right
quarters. When, therefore, he was appointed
Solicitor-General in 1915 nobody was very much surprised, and certainly nobody was shocked. He was
adequate to the duties, and not more than adequate :
the sort of man who, in quiet times, climbs step by
step to the highest positions without anybody being
able to say why he should be there or why not.

The war, however, brought Sir Stanley Buckmaster
duties which demanded a certain human quality
which he lacks. The volatile Sir F. E. Smith, after
a brief experience of the post of Chief Censor, decided
to go to France, and a thankless job was handed
over to the Solicitor-General. It is quite possible
that the historian will attach a good deal of importance to this appointment; it certainly had much
influence on the course of events. It may be doubted
whether Sir Stanley Buckmaster went to the Press
Bureau with any policy of his own; more probably
he stolidly pursued the policy he found there. That
policy was one of quite stupid suppression. The
public was kept for six months in almost complete
ignorance of facts, and became a prey, first, to a
senseless optimism, and, next to something closely
resembling panic. One important result is directly
traceable to Sir Stanley Buckmaster's exaggeration
of "reticence." A certain kind of newspaper, foiled
in all attempts to get itself talked about and sold
through its news columns, made the experiment of
importing sensation into its hitherto neglected leading
article. Since it could not retail news from the
front, it would make news at home. The experiment
was, from its special point of view, a brilliant success.
The country was convulsed; nothing else was talked
about; even Lord Kitchener's prestige was shaken;
whole groups of officials and Ministers were displaced;
and the lesson was learned in Fleet Street that it
is sometimes better business to make history than

to chronicle it. What has since been attacked as "newspaper government" springs from that simple discovery.

The explosion of public feeling in the spring of 1915 did no immediate injury to the Minister whose concealment of facts largely provoked it. Indeed, it actually led to brilliant promotion. Victims must be found, and who more appropriate than Lord Haldane, who had said Germany was his spiritual home? Lord Haldane, overwhelmed by the storm, left the Woolsack; Baron Buckmaster of Cheddington was called into existence as his successor. He continued to be Lord Chancellor until the next change of Administration, when the proprieties demanded that a "Unionist" should replace him. Hence it arrives that the country is paying thirty thousand a year for one giant of the law who is not overworked and for four who are burdened with no duties at all. And yet a Lord Chancellor has no necessary connection with war or party politics!

Lord Buckmaster's active career quite possibly ended with his resignation at the end of 1916. For men of his particular stamp the future will probably hold fewer opportunities than the past. But he is not on that account negligible. In his detachment he has developed the malady which seems to attack distinguished lawyers in retreat, and with Lord Loreburn he is treading the rather slippery path that leads to Lansdowne House. At any rate, he is approaching very closely to that school which accepts President Wilson as idealist and rejects him as realist. Lord Buckmaster is quite sure that there must be a League of Nations; he is far from sure that the defeat of Imperialist Germany is an essential condition of the success of such a League.

There was once an "exhorter" on the Western plains who prayed that a notorious sinner might be bitten by a rattlesnake, on the ground that "nothing

but rattlesnakes would bring Jake to repentance."
Germany's case is much the same. The nation has
been so systematically infected with the virus of
Prussianism that nothing short of the imminent threat
of national death will effect a cure. The German
Socialists admitted that Lenin and Trotsky, by their
non-resistance, had made the position of the German
peace party not less but more difficult. "We cannot," they said in so many words, "place ourselves
in the position of critics of so great a German success." It can be inferred what would be the effect
of weak compromise on the part of the other Powers.
Anything short of the complete bankruptcy of the
Prussian system will leave it all-powerful in Germany, and therefore capable of resuming in due
course the policy which Prussia has followed consistently since the days of the Great Elector. To a
still Prussianized German Empire the League of
Nations would simply be a greater opportunity for
intrigue than its Bismarcks have ever enjoyed; it
would be merely an extended Concert of Europe.

Surrender is an ugly word. But when we have
volatilized all the noble sentiment and seeming reasonableness of Lansdowneism, surrender is the only solid
thing left in the test-tube. It may be an injustice
to suggest that Lord Buckmaster and Lord Loreburn
are taking the Lansdowneward course. But these
are days in which men must be very careful of the
company they keep.

MR. SAMUEL GOMPERS

" I AM an internationalist, but my doctrine is an
addition and not a subtraction. I must be a citizen
of America before I can be a citizen of the world."

These are the words of Mr. Samuel Gompers,
President and to a great extent creator of that powerful organization, the American Federation of Labour.
They are the more remarkable when we bear in mind
the sort of man Mr. Gompers is. Superficially he
should have all the makings of a "citizen of the
world," and it is not so obvious why he should be
first and foremost an American patriot. He is of
Jewish race. He is of Dutch and French ancestry.
He was not even American born. Like Mr. Hughes,
of Australia, he first saw the light as it is dulled down
by the eternal murk of poorer London. It was in the
East End that he lived till he was thirteen—a typical
child of the London ghetto, undersized, overnerved,
sharp and avid as the sparrow of the gutters. His
father worked in the cigar trade; there was no better
opening for the boy, and when the paternal Gompers
went to New York young Samuel followed the family
occupation. He was soon expert as a cigar-roller,
and even now, after the lapse of more than half a
century, his fingers have not forgotten their cunning.

There is one advantage—if it can be reckoned
such—in manual work of this type. It makes little
demand on the brain. One can think as one works.
One's mind is free if one's hand is a slave. In the
cigar shop—it was hardly a factory—where young
Gompers was employed, the workers whiled away
the tedious hours by reading to one another. Gompers, who had even in those days an emphatic and
distinct delivery, was generally employed as reader.

It was much such an atmosphere as that which determined the future of Charles Dickens. The boy's literary taste rapidly developed; and the desultory acquirements of the shop were amplified by a more systematic attack on the classics during scanty hours of leisure. Gompers devoured the English novelists. Then, tiring of fiction, he turned his attention to John Stuart Mill and the professors of the dismal science generally. It was perhaps lucky that he started with the individualists; the German Socialists and Henry George had less effect on his mind when he reached them. It may be questioned, however, whether he would in any circumstances have rendered an unquestioning homage to that school. For he was from the first of a wholly practical turn, and far more interested in the world, and especially that part of the world in which he found himself, than in any Utopia.

It is unnecessary for the present purpose to follow the career of Mr. Gompers in detail, or to trace step by step the process by which he built up, from quite small beginnings, the organization which now wields gigantic power in every part of the United States and bargains with capital in the name of three million men. But it is important to understand what is roughly the basis of his authority. Mr. Gompers has done many things which would be considered "advanced" even by our own Syndicalists. But the Federation is in no sense a revolutionary organization. It does not exist for promoting class war or social unrest; it is a machine contrived to attain most definite and concrete ends. Mr. Gompers himself regards a strike as evidence of failure. He believes in negotiation, and in having a case so strong as to compel agreement on the part of the opposing party. He is about as far removed from the usual conception of an agitator as can well be imagined—a man of singularly orderly mind, almost painfully correct in his diction, as cool as Rockefeller or any of the Big Five, pliable as to indifferent matters, inflexible on essentials. In its methods the American Federation of Labour, in fact, strikingly resembles the great financial corporations it has to deal with. It is a thoroughly businesslike institution, and its President is as keen, as cautious, if need be as ruthless, as the president of any trust, but withal as ready to see the opposing point of view and to do a "deal" without reference to any social or political prejudice.

Such is the man—shrewd, hard-headed, practical. His work has presented special difficulties of a kind not easy to be grasped on this side of the Atlantic. There is a wide difference between British and American labour conditions. Here, after all, labour is mainly British; foreign infiltration affects only a few large towns, and even in the capital does not materially modify the character of the population. In America, on the other hand, the "Anglo-Saxon" workman—even if we include the Irishman—is something of a rarity. An enormous amount of the hard work of the great Republic is done by miscellaneous foreigners; even Germans are a minority among the great crowd recruited from every backward monarchy in Europe. Among these men general education is defective, and they speak very poor English. The more intelligent of them bear a grudge against civilization, and have no special reason to be attached to the institutions of the United States. The control of a body which includes great masses of men of this class should, one would imagine, be far more difficult than the task of British Labour leaders, and when war came to inflame racial and national differences it seemed a bold thing on Mr. Gompers's part to answer for the solidarity of American organized labour.

That the claim was no idle one, however, has been proved by events. There have been troubles between employer and employed, but, on the whole, astonishingly few, and those which have occurred have been settled with extraordinary facility through machinery of Mr. Gompers's own devising. He has worked with the President as Marshal Haig with Marshal Foch. The debt the United States, and the Allies in general, owe to this remarkable man is beyond doubt enormous. In acknowledging it we may usefully enquire why Mr. Gompers occupies a position so far removed from that of those of our own Labour leaders who specially retain control of the " machine." Why is he " out " to beat Germany, and not, like Mr. Henderson, " out " only to get victory for the " international proletariat "? Mr. Gompers is a lifelong pacifist, just as Mr. Henderson is. He has been much nearer the proletariat than Mr. Henderson ever was. He has fought such fights for Labour as Mr. Henderson's meeker nature would have shunned. He is only an American by adoption. Mr. Henderson's ancestor probably drew a good bow at Hastings. Why, then, does Mr. Gompers, instead of courting the German Socialists like Mr. Henderson, repeat in every speech, a veritable American Cato, " Germany must be beaten; the war must be fought to victory "?

The question is answered by Mr. Gompers himself in the words quoted above: " I must be a citizen of America before I can be a citizen of the world." Perhaps the coarsest of all the mistakes made by Germany was with regard to the reality of American citizenship. Germany laid stress on the ethnic factor, and it is no doubt a considerable element in American life. It gives all kinds of Americans, for example, a curiously tired feeling when they read our well-meant eulogies on themselves and their institutions. A nation which derives from every race in Europe is not likely to be flattered when we assume that its main duty is to " take its stand by the Mother Country for the preservation of the common interest of Anglo-Saxondom "—which, .it seems, includes India, West Africa, and the Hokojoko Islands. America does not happen to be "Anglo-Saxon," even if we are. But though America is not English (except as regards the bases of law and language), America is American. With America neutral, personal and racial preferences assumed extraordinary warmth, and took the most lawless form. But with America belligerent, the ranks have closed marvellously.

To what are we to attribute a general loyalty hardly equalled in any European country? Something is due, no doubt, to the peculiar directness of the American intellect, which is as sharply distinguishable from our own habit of cloudy compromise as the thoroughgoing heat and cold of the American continent are from our trimming climate. Still more, no doubt, is traceable to the school system of the United States, which brings vivid and even crude Americanism into the homes of Italian, Hungarian, Galician, Scandinavian, and German parents. But in the long run the most powerful influence is the democratic and Republican temper which, if it does not kill the spirit of sectionalism, at least scotches it. The immense bulk of the United States does not prevent an intense localism. Every American has his "home town," as well as his home State, and it thus results that the most cosmopolitan community on earth is also the least international. Mr. Gompers's citizen formula might be extended thus: "I am first of all a citizen of Big Lick; I am next a citizen of the State of Missouri; I am next a citizen of the United States; and after that (when I have time) I am a citizen of the world." "What do they know of England," asks Mr. Kipling, "who England only know?" A much more reasonable question is, What can they feel for the British Empire who decry either their native Buluwayo or their native Chipping Sodbury? British Imperialism has made

one mistake in seeking to turn Englishmen and
Scotchmen into Britishers. British Labour has made
another in trying to regard itself as part of the " international proletariat." Both have begun at the
wrong end. One can be a good Englishman first,
and all sorts of things afterwards—enthusiastic for
the British Commonwealth, and friendly to the League
of Nations. One cannot safely reverse the process,
and that we exist at all to-day is due to the splendid
fact that the average Englishman, Scotsman, and
Welshman, despite all exhortations to think imperially
and proletarianly, insisted at the critical moment on
thinking nationally.

In this context it is highly significant that, while
there is a colossal Labour organization in America,
there is no Labour Party in Congress. Mr. Gompers
has set his face like flint against all pressure to form
one, and has declined all invitations to be nominated
himself. He thinks " the welfare of Labour should
not be confused with other national interests, but
should be the concern of all parties." This pure
wisdom does not, of course, prevent the American
Labour organization from bringing strong and successful pressure to bear on all kinds of matters in
which the working man is specially interested. In
fact, Mr. Gompers has taken an enormous part in
State and Federal politics. But, like the millionaires
themselves, he recognizes the indecency of open sectionalism under a democratic institution. It is something altogether repellent to the national temper.
Class interests exist in America as elsewhere, and are
pursued with equal selfishness. But the point is that
the sectionalist is forced by public sentiment to clothe
his sordidness with at least the show of public spirit.

The British Labour Party cannot be blamed because, coming late in the day, and finding nakedly
selfish parties in possession, it has fought for its own
hand. It could scarcely do otherwise. But when it

is beginning to aspire to control national destiny it should seek larger models, and since there is little indeed to copy at home, it would do better to turn to Mr. Gompers and American Labour than to Trotsky and Russian Bolshevism, or to "our German friends," whether they follow Scheidemann or Haase.

THE END